THE PERFECT
TREEHOUSE

from site selection
to design & construction

DJANGO KRONER

POPULAR WOODWORKING BOOKS

CINCINNATI, OHIO

popularwoodworking.com

D1205145

THE PERFECT TREEHOUSE

from site selection
to design & construction

DJANGO KRONER

contents

preface

I felt a distinct clash of confusion and wonder when I woke up. I couldn't recall where I was and didn't know what time of night it was. I was surrounded above and below by thousands of tiny blinking lights and there was a loud pulsing choir of chirps and clicks. I yawned and exhaled into the thick air of an approaching fog. I sat up in my hammock, and focused out into the darkness. It was at this precise moment that I was hit with a rush of contentment. Like sitting down in your most comfortable chair after hours of hard labor, I felt like I had accomplished my mission or found a secret destination I had been searching for. In my heightened state I recognized the fireflies and spring peeper that captivated my senses at night in these woods. I was surrounded in 360° by these creatures and felt like guest in their home. I was spending the first night of many, forty-five feet up, in my newly built treehouse in Kentucky's Red River Gorge.

I had moved to the gorge about four months earlier. I was nineteen years old and yearned to connect with the area and test my skills as a rock climber. The gorge is gifted with Corbin sandstone cliffs and lush rainforest-like hillsides. It's a true rock climbing paradise east of the Mississippi. I moved there with little other plan than to become a stronger rock climber and apprentice with a timber-frame cabin builder in exchange for room and board. My goals were simple and time was abundant. I would spend hours in the hot sun chiseling mortises, and then head to the cliffs as the temperatures dropped. I would climb until sunset, hike home, cook a feast and then go to bed. It wasn't long until I realized that the bunkhouse in the parking lot was not the natural setting I was seeking for my bedroom. I pitched a tent back in the woods and laid awake much of the night wondering what it was that had just knocked over my water bottle. Still, I enjoyed the solitude and the weeks flew by. We had constructed the first of three floors of a giant timber-beam cabin, and I started to understand a little about how much patience is needed to be a good timber-frame craftsman. I was pleased with my setting, and was determined to stay the course as long as I had my chance to climb.

June came and with it all of the perks of summer in a jungle. Rain, humidity, mold, bugs and snakes had become my frequent roommates in my nylon tent. My boots developed a squish and eerie black mold grew quickly across the logo on my rain fly. I held high spirits, but they were mostly a cover for decreasing motivation. I wanted so badly to connect with this place, to prove my dedication, and to learn whatever it was I couldn't get from a mere weekend camping trip. I thought my best route was to just keep at it, but building was starting to feel like work. And as for climbing, my grip on the steep sandstone was slipping as sweat infiltrated the creases between my fingers. Life had become just plain sticky.

One morning after a rainy night, I woke up to a flooded tent and wet sleeping mat. I unzipped my screen, swiveled my feet out of the door and grabbed my boots to slide them on. I was greeted by a copperhead that had decided to take up residence. Luckily, I saw the snake in time and promptly threw the boot in the air as it slithered out of my toe cap. I collapsed back on my wet tent in defeat. As I lay there I watched the sun peak through and scare the clouds away. I noticed how the breeze ruffled the leaves of the tall tulip poplars. I felt the dank, dark air of the forest floor against my chest while I watched the tops of trees light up from the suns ray's. I was in awe at how majestic the pale blue sky looked through the filter of the big leaf magnolia leaves. At that moment, I realized that I absolutely, without a doubt, needed to move into the trees.

Have you ever been eating breakfast and all of the sudden remembered a delightful idea you had in a dream the night before? That's what that moment felt like. Building a treehouse wasn't exactly a new dream of mine. When I was a kid I would spend hours a day alone in the treetops. I would watch videos of orangutans and try to mimic their movement to better my climbing. I would climb trees to escape the wrath of my older brother, and I always felt safe in the limbs of a sugar maple. Like most kids, treehouses ignited one of the deepest wells of my imagination. I suppose, as I grew older this dream was put on the back burner and it wasn't until that day, somewhere between being a carefree kid and an adult, that I remembered my dream. It felt comfortable and it felt like home.

That day at lunch I hiked back to my site and began exploring the canopy with my eyes. I saw a collection of hemlocks, big leaf magnolias, white oaks, sycamores and poplars. I took note of how thick they were and how far apart they were from one another. I knew that a treehouse is only as grand as its host, and I knew that choosing the trees was going to be a very difficult decision. I spent each night in the office researching how to build treehouses and how trees grew, and looking at treehouses for inspiration. About two months passed until one night the perfect trees popped out to me. I saw the sycamore and tulip poplar that straddled the creek at the valley floor. I liked the idea of sleeping above running water and that the trees sat perpendicular to the direction of the holler. This meant I would have an unobstructed view. I began sketching designs, trying to determine what the simplest version possible would look like. I knew I wanted as much exposure to the canopy as I could get while remaining comfortable and safe. I knew I wanted to be to be high to achieve the best view possible. I had virtually no budget and knew that using scrap materials was going to be key to my success. Later that week I had come up with my final design. I ordered wood from the local saw mill, and convinced some climbing buddies to come over that weekend to help me start hauling beams to my build site in the woods.

I climbed the sycamore trunk first. I used a primitive aid system that was slow but did the trick. I then set safety and rigging lines that hung between the two trees. With my background in climbing, I considered the rope work to be the easy part. It was the construction that would be my challenge. I had just finished a year of Ameri-Corps building houses with Habitat for Humanity, so I had a decent idea of what building a house took. I designed my treehouse to hang on cables, so that the trees could have room to sway in the wind and grow. I drilled a 1" hole through the trunk of each tree and hammered a 1" pipe to act as a sleeve in the hole. Then I threaded ½" aircraft cable through the pipe that extended down to beams on either side of the trees. Once I framed the rectangle that hung level around the trees I was able to raise a platform frame I built on the ground and set it onto the beams. Progress was slow. All of my help was volunteered so I would only get a few boards up at a time, usually in the evening after everyone was already worn out from the day's activities.

Once I had a flat surface to stand on I could feel my dream becoming close to reality. I was brimming with excitement, and as soon as I tacked down enough decking to sleep on, I moved up! I wore a harness the first few nights until the deck was big enough that I was sure I wouldn't roll off. I made a fifty-foot rope ladder out of old climbing rope and beech limbs, and instead of having a lock or a door, I spaced the rungs two feet apart, which deterred your average passer by from intrusion. My treehouse was 10' x 12'. It had a roof and railing, but no walls to block me from my treetop view. I knew that as I grew older, amenities would become priority, so I took advantage of this time to seek maximum exposure. It was simple, small, and full of flaws, but I woke up every morning with a huge smile and sense of pride. I had built the perfect vehicle to start me on the canopy lifestyle I was destined for.

I lived in that treehouse for three years. Flying squirrels, tree frogs, and luna moths visited me. I heard barred owls meet late in the night and I woke up unable to see the ground as I floated above the morning fog. Spending that time in the trees exposed me to a magic that I hadn't felt since I was a young kid. No matter what my day dealt me, by the time I reached the last rung of the rope ladder I was laughing to myself at how lucky I was. Getting to know my treehouse inspired me. I learned to hike the trail backwards so I could see my friends' faces the first time they looked up and saw my treehouse. It seemed to bring out the kid in everyone – the kind of kid that doesn't know any better than to just chase their dreams. The way my treehouse inspired people totally sealed the deal for me; I knew what I wanted to do with my life. I wanted to share the canopy experience with my friends and family. I want treehouses to inspire others as they have inspired me. That is when I decided to start the Canopy Crew, and that is when I fully dedicated myself to learning about tree health and treehouse building.

introduction

When I built my first treehouse I did as much research as I could. I ran laps around the Internet, read Peter Nelson's treehouse books, and exhausted my mind trying to find out what problems I might encounter along the way. I reached a point when I realized I was just going to have to go for it. I made a lot of mistakes. Not just on the first one either; as I built a second treehouse and a third, I would realize mistakes I made and learn from them. I am grateful for these mistakes. For me, a portfolio of mistakes and corrections is so much more valuable than a few builds where everything went smoothly. I now know (so much more than I did before) the importance of having a plan and following certain rules to protect the trees. What's the point of building a treehouse if you don't treat your foundation with utmost respect and care? I have infected a tree with a fungal disease. I have used poor rigging techniques that resulted in large beams falling out of the sky. I have even had to raise entire structures to swap out foundation beams to allow for more tree growth. Through these experiences I have learned so much, and I always keep to the beginner's mind. No matter how far down the treehouse path you go, there are infinite ways to improve your skill set and knowledge. A large part of this is due to the fact that every tree is different. Not only from species to species, but from one individual to the next.

Guys like Peter Nelson, Charlie Greenwood and Michael Garnier are true pioneers of arboreal building. (Nelson's books provide me with endless inspiration.) They have been out there paving the way for the rest of us and have taken years of experience to the shop to create hardware and products that are taking treehouse building to the next level. We are on the brink of a treehouse explosion, which is really exiting because not only will thousands of people bask in the glory of canopy living, but thousands will make mistakes, improve upon design and techniques, and ultimately push the limits of the treehouse world. I cannot wait to see what's in store for treehouses!

There are a few books out there that teach you how to build treehouses. They make great points and touch on a lot of fundamentals. What I have learned through my experience is that treehouse building is complex, because trees are complex. You simply cannot make sweeping

My first treehouse was simple, small and full of flaws, but it was the perfect vehicle to start me on the canopy lifestyle I was destined for.

statements about trees because they vary so much. Just like humans, what is healthy for one, could kill the next. I have found that these books lack detail. They explain one scenario, but don't give you the tools for problem solving when you are out in the woods facing a whole new set of obstacles. They also focus on construction, and leave out important aspects of tree climbing, tree health and rigging. Believe me, getting a building square on the ground is one thing, but getting it square up in the air while hanging in a harness is completely different.

The goal of this book is to help you avoid the mistakes that others have made as you build your own treehouse. This book will provide you with answers to questions, examples of successful and unsuccessful builds, and technical details of how to get the job done. It will cover all areas of treehouse building such as tree selection and care, tree climbing, design and rigging, mistakes to avoid, and construction. Personally, I cannot just read a textbook and absorb the information effectively. Everyone learns in his or her own way and it is my goal to lay out the technical aspects of treehouse building using several different ways of explanation and teaching. I set out to write the book that I wished I had when I got started. My aim is to give you the tools to be a good treehouse builder, not just a book on how to build one good treehouse.

Treehouses, by nature, are wild. There is something about climbing a tree and making a home in it that is primitive, beautiful and rebellious. To commit your home, or even just a side project, to a living being that will react to your presence and one day die is a profound way to go about construction! Similar to the artwork of Andy Goldsworthy, the uniqueness of a treehouse is the fact that it's built within and alongside nature. There is something almost piratical and against the grain about treehouses and it's important to keep this in mind as you read this book. To build a treehouse, you must harness the spirit of "just going for it." This book is not meant to tame the act of treetop building, because it can't be done. Take your yearning to make a home amongst boughs and branches, use this book as a guide and tool in your toolbox, and enjoy the adventure!

I spent three years living in my treehouse in Kentucky's Red River Gorge. When it comes to treehouses, location means everything. Where will you build yours?

PLANNING YOUR TREEHOUSE

location

Before you select your trees, you must have an inspirational location. Not everyone has choices. You may have one small tree in your backyard and three kids tugging at your pant legs begging for a treehouse. Or you may have a whole forest to choose from. When building on the ground, it's easier to imagine the view and perspective of a house before it's built. This isn't always the case when you're building in trees. The other reality is that a house is generally designed to hide you away from the outside. Whereas a treehouse is all about being up in the tree! A treehouse is all about exposing you to a whole new world and enjoying the view below. Placement and orientation are the first steps to deciding the aesthetic of your treehouse. It's wise to pick a few options for location and weigh the pros and cons – then see what you are working with in terms of tree species and tree selection.

One of the easiest mistakes to make pre-build is being overconfident or forgetful about your rigging skills when selecting a site. Yes, that is a beautiful stand of white oaks perched on top of the cliff, but will you really be able to get 200-pound beams up there? And will you be able to afford to pay the labor to get them up in the tree once you have figured out how to do it? I am all for choosing the most epic build site, but being realistic and keeping things simple is important for seeing the project through to the end.

When I built my first treehouse, which I call the "ape escape," I started climbing with a general plan of placing the foundation at twenty feet. I had so much fun climbing and seeing the view for the first time I ended up getting forty-five feet up before I stopped and decided to drill. Looking back, I am so happy I built and lived that high, because the view was amazing! The valley sloped downward so it really felt like I was above the forest. At the same time, this simple fact probably added several weeks and gallons of sweat to the build. Not to mention I had a few very scary nights where the winds were making my host trees sway eight feet side to side. Height off of the ground will determine a lot about how you build and how the house will feel when you're up there. Better views often mean more movement of the structure and more difficulty getting into the house. I loved the elevation and exposure of mine, but it wasn't for everyone and there were moments I wished I had built a second level closer to the ground.

It may sound obvious, but running through a checklist when deciding upon location can save you valuable time and effort. Here is a list of questions you should ask yourself while searching for a build site:

1. Can you drive to the location?
2. If not, how far is the hike to the site?
3. With the length of that hike, and the dimensions of the lumber you will need, will you be able to carry all of the construction materials needed to the location?
4. How far is the nearest available electricity?
5. Does the terrain pose potential for disaster (such as erosion, lightning, landslides or flooding)?
6. Based on first impressions, are there suitable, healthy trees to build in that will get you the view and feel you want?

A more site-specific set of questions arises based on where you live. Making sure you are indeed on your property and are going to be able to build within the limits of your local zoning and codes is important. Building codes and permits are a tricky subject because more often than not there simply aren't any codes written specifically about treehouses. While I highly recommend doing your homework on your local codes, there are no blanket answers regarding rules. Codes vary for every state, city and county. Often times if you're building small – under 200 square feet, for example – your building won't be held to many of the codes that exist. Building a certain distance from your property line and keeping your neighbors' privacy in mind is, of course, the right thing to do. I would certainly avoid building a treehouse that can be used to look into your neighbor's windows. If you are building in an urban area, I believe the most important step is getting permission from your neighbors. If you have a neighbor that will complain and report you to the city, then getting your treehouse off the ground can become a huge headache. Plan your structure well with safety in mind, and you will have a much easier time talking with the inspector about your treehouse. Look up your local standards of framing and follow them. There are rules about side structures and you can usually easily follow them to ensure that your treehouse isn't going to be considered illegal. Sometimes there are rules about height off of the ground, posts in the ground or maximum roof height. If you want to be bulletproof, follow the rules closely. I recommend finding an engineer and architect to help you along the way. I know of one specialist at treehouseengineering.com who should be able to assist anyone interested in pursing permits and stamps. The best option is to build in an area that allows for treehouses and total creative freedom.

tree selection

Undoubtedly the most important step in building your treehouse is choosing the trees to build in. You could tackle any obstacle to build an amazing treehouse in the best location only to find out that the species you selected has weak heartwood and cannot support your treehouse. Just like any building, the structure will only be as strong as its foundation. This is why you want to choose trees that not only inspire you, but also are some of the best options you have in terms of species and individual tree selection.

The first pitfall of tree selection is canopy fever: You're super excited about your new build. You've got your location picked out; you're standing there looking at the most beautiful old growth tree on your property. It all clicks. This is the one! This tree has it all: a large trunk, perfectly rounded crown, lush foliage and a great view from its perch. You know you have to build in this tree. It's the perfect tree! You go grab your drill...

At this time it's best to take a step back – you are about to start down a road where you simply cannot predict the destination. I know all too well the feeling of canopy fever. The excitement is overwhelming. Rushing into your tree–treehouse relationship is never a good idea. First you must do your research, assess the tree, and talk to a local arborist to make sure you really are building in the best host tree. This step takes time. Things can move slowly when dealing with a consulting service. But it is important to remember that tree species, tree quality and tree location come into play when assessing your tree. There is no perfect tree type. What may be great in the West could terrible in the East. What could be strong and viable in your neighbor's yard could be weak and compromised in your yard where you just put in a new retaining wall. For example, ash trees would be suitable hosts in the western United States, but all across the Midwest they are stricken with the emerald ash borer (an invasive beetle killing off all of the ash trees). A reputable International Society of Arboriculture (ISA) certified arborist could look at your trees and discover signs of struggle that may be invisible to the average homeowner. If there is an arborist in your location, then you really should take advantage of their skills. I would even recommend getting multiple opinions. Often times an arborist will do a visual inspection of your tree for free. Getting their approval of health is a great first step on your way to building.

If you have selected trees that inspire you and fit your vision for building, here are a few steps to take on your own to help determine if they would make good hosts.

1. Look at the ground. What is the soil around the tree like? Does the tree stand in a stable location?
2. Do the root crown or runner roots suffer from compaction? Typical causes may be a nearby driveway, sidewalk, construction project or heavy foot traffic.
3. Are there any holes at the base or trunk of tree? Is there any rot, decay, fungus or saw dust at the base of the tree?
4. Does the trunk sound hollow when you kick it with a sturdy pair of boots?
5. Does the crown of the tree looked balanced? Are there any forks in the tree that look like they are collecting water or are split? Are the main crotches of the tree really narrow or wide?
6. Are the tips of the branches dead through a large portion of the crown?
7. Is there any lightning or storm damage visible from the ground?
8. Does the tree have the same amount of foliage as any neighboring trees of the same species?

If the tree looks in good shape from the ground, the next step is to climb it and check it out from a more intimate setting. From above you can see into the crotches of the tree and really see if there is any rotting or splitting. You can also get a much closer look at the tips of the branches to see if there are any issues with dieback (this is where the tips of a branch failed to produce new buds, and it is a sign of suffering). Climbing your tree is great fun and I will discuss how to climb safely and efficiently in chapter three.

For the most part, if a tree looks sick, it probably isn't a good choice to build in. Certain trees are more like weeds than trees: they grow fast and are ugly and nearly impossible to kill. Some trees are slow growing and beautiful but have sensitive immune systems. Going through a checklist is the first step when reviewing your chosen tree. Next, you can identify the tree species and look up their strengths and weaknesses. Things to check out are lifespan, qualities of the lumber from that tree type, how the tree reacts to pruning, and if there are any plagues or diseases in your area for that species. It is important to know that trees don't heal, they compartmentalize. This is a process where trees will quarantine a rot area and close off the healthy tissue from it. You can see this anywhere a branch has been cut, look for rounded edges that look like lips. Some trees are better at compartmentalization than others and its good to avoid trees that are notoriously bad. Each climate has its own struggles. For example, the hemlock wooly adelgid beetle has ravaged the Red River Gorge in Kentucky. So hemlocks are out of the question as trees for treehouses. In the Midwest, ash trees have the emerald ash borer, so they are no longer viable. Dutch elm disease has made its way across the continent over the past hundred years! At times it may seem like trees are doomed, but remember that nature has cycles that have been going on since the beginning of time. As someone who works in trees for a living, I have concluded that trees are very resilient. Take one look at a tree grown under a power line and you will see that trees find a way. Pests and fungi may kill trees as much as urban expansion, but finding a great tree is all about doing a little site-specific research. Find a tree that you like and learn about it. Weigh the pros and cons of using it as a host tree. Each tree will have positives and negatives. Red oaks have extremely strong lumber and thick trunks, but they are prone to blowing over in a strong wind. Sycamores have irresistible white canopies, but are sensitive to fungal diseases carried on metal tools. Sometimes you have to work with what you have, and that is OK. For me, I like having limited choices because it takes away the questioning. This is the tree I have to work with; I will design and create to fit the tree. It is fun when you have a funky branch to work around, or a big burl in the way of your framing. Character in the tree provides a nice building challenge!

While I am not a believer in sweeping statements about "good trees" and "bad trees," here is a rough list of trees ranked by quality as hosts (specific to the Midwestern United States):

QUALITY HOSTS	DECENT HOSTS	POOR HOSTS
white oak	sycamore	silver maple
hickory	walnut	cottonwood
fir	poplar	box elder
pine	red oak	ash
maple	mulberry	hemlock
apple	locust	
spruce	beech	
osage		
cypress		

One of my mentors, Ron Rothhaas, has been studying trees since before I was born. Here is his "homeowner's advice" to tree assessment for selecting a good treehouse tree.

When I walk up to a tree the first thing I look for is a good full canopy, with healthy looking leaves. There should be no fungal growth or dead areas in the trunk or main branches. If there is fungal growth, I assess what type it is and find out how aggressive it is and if it's treatable. Ganoderma is a huge red flag. This is a lethal, untreatable fungus that attacks the roots of the tree and can cause structural failure. Wide-angle crotches are stronger than narrow crotches. I would look at the tree type and find out if it is good at compartmentalization or not. For example, white oak and hickory trees are great, where as red oak and beech aren't as good. Ultimately, I would never trust an uneducated assessment. Have your tree looked at not only by an ISA-certified arborist but also by a Tree Risk Assessment Qualification (TRAQ) arborist. Someone with this education will specialize in the structural stability of a tree, which is really what you want to check for before

building in it. As a homeowner, you can tap the tree with a mallet to listen for hollow sounds in the trunk. A qualified professional can go as far as performing a resistograph test on the tree, which measures the amount of decay in the trunk. It is important to use sharp tools when drilling into a tree. Sharp edges cut tissue and encourage compartmentalization as opposed to tearing, which can leave the tree exposed. Once you invest in your trees, there is an element of ongoing care. Have your trees inspected a year after your build and every two years from there on out. Avoid soil compaction around the tree. In a yard, use mulch to mitigate compaction and improve biological balances. In the forest, use leaf litter around the base, taking advantage of the natural humus. Use a 50/50 blend of compost to biochar (charcoal used as a soil additive) to give the trees an advantage. In areas of extreme compaction, for example right after construction, an aeration knife can break up the soil around the roots. I would also recommend using a tree growth regulator after you drill into a tree. Trees produce their own chemicals that regulate growth (mostly at the tips). A tree growth regulator short-circuits that process and redirects the carbohydrates to focus on compartmentalization and other healing. A tree growth regulator will slow the growth of the tree but not slow the process of photosynthesis. With the regulator, trees are better able to withstand drought or respond to any damage done during construction. An arborist in tune with your local habitat will be best fitted to diagnose your trees.

Ronald E. Rothhaas, Jr.

Arbor Doctor, LLC

www.arbordoctor.com

Member, American Society of Consulting Arborists, International Society of Arboriculture

ISA Certified Arborist, OH-5177A

ISA Tree Risk Assessment Qualification

B.S. Horticulture Interpretation, The Ohio State University

A.A.B. Ornamental Horticulture, Cincinnati State Technical and Community College

The bottom line with tree selection is to do your homework. Whether you know it or not, you will develop a relationship with the trees you build in. There is a level of gamble with tree selection but knowing you did your research and knowing you care about your trees will take away the stress. The trees you build in are an investment. There is a level of ongoing care you'll need to commit to. Even if it's just simply taking time to look at the new growth of the tree and examining the tree for compartmentalization or rot. As mentioned in the sidebar, I recommend having your arborist do a follow up a year after you build and every two years after that.

tree climbing

Climbing a tree for the first time is an honor. Checking things out from above for the first time is always motivating. Not only will you likely have to climb the tree to get access to your build site, but you will also have to set safety and rigging lines, and do an inspection of the canopy. There are many ways to climb a tree. You can use a ladder, you can free-solo up the branches without a rope, or you can set a line and climb it like a professional arborist. How you climb your tree is a personal choice, but I will teach the way of an arborist. One thing is certain: You should not put on a pair of climbing spurs and spike up your soon to be host. Spiking up living trees is an old practice. You should only wear spurs if you are planning on cutting the tree down.

Any type of climbing is inherently risky. Any decision you make when climbing your tree must be ultimately your own. This chapter will explain the basics of tree climbing, but never hesitate to hire a professional to climb and inspect your tree or set rigging lines. Tree climbing is an activity that takes years to master and any time you enter the vertical world you should be alert. Respect gravity. Rule number one of tree climbing is to trust your gut. If it doesn't feel right, don't do it. Rule number two is wear a helmet. You may not ever fall climbing, but if your rope snaps a dead limb out from above, the branch can fall with a vengeance. I have taken hits to the helmet from branches only 2" in diameter that were painful enough for me to know that I never want to experience that on my bare skull.

What to have in your bare-bones tree-climbing backpack:

- Harness: many types will do but a tree-climbing harness will be the most comfortable and easiest to use
- Tree-climbing rope: not a rock-climbing rope (it's not designed for high friction and is too stretchy), not a rigging-rope (it's too bulky and is not stretchy enough), not a sailing rope (it's not designed for high friction and is not stretchy enough)
- Throw line
- Helmet
- Flipline or lanyard
- Spliced split tail

- Micro pulley
- Two locking carabiners

If your tree has branches you can reach, but you still want to have a rope on, then you can use a flipline to always stay secured to the tree. This is a system where you have a harness and two lanyards. A lanyard – also known as a flipline – is basically a rope that goes from one hip, around the tree, and attaches to the other hip. This way if you slip, the rope will catch you. Once you are in the tree, you can alternate from one lanyard to the next to make upward progress and always stay attached. You are still using your arms and legs to advance upward, but the lanyard is keeping you safe. You should always weight each flipline *before* undoing your last one. This way you know it is set up around a branch that will hold. Tree-climbing fliplines are designed so that you can take in or let out slack as needed. This is useful if you are moving to a branch that is farther away than your hips can reach.

If your tree doesn't have lower branches, then you will need to set a climbing line in the tree so that you can ascend the line and gain access to the canopy. This is great fun and will make you feel like a pro right off the bat. To set a climbing line in the tree, you must send a throw line over the branch or crotch you choose as your anchor. A throw line is a thin line with a beanbag on the end. You throw the beanbag over the crotch and let it fall back to the ground. Then you tie on your climbing line and pull the throw line up and over, providing you with a top rope to climb off of. Select a strong crotch; centrally located high in the canopy, that has a downward pull on the branch it comes from.

If you are like me and are not good at throwing a ball, you can use a specialized slingshot to shoot the ball (also a fun game for after hours). Once you get your climbing line into the tree, bounce test it. Put your full weight on the rope and jump up and down multiple times to make sure the crotch you are in is strong enough to hold you. It is better to snap out a branch and fall two feet onto the ground than to snap it out from higher up, so don't be afraid to really bounce hard on your rope. As you bounce test, look down the limbs that hold up your branch to see if there are any splits or cracks. Before you decide its safe, think to yourself, "Would I hang my grandma on this rope?"

Now that your rope is set and you have decided it is a strong anchor, you can ascend the line. There are many ways to do this; rock climbers, arborists and cavers all have their own versions with different sets of gear. I will teach you a way that is tried and true (and cost effective). If you want to climb trees a lot, I highly recommend doing some research and buying a mechanical rope ascender. This will save your arms and be much faster than going the old-school route. The method I teach in this book is nice because you don't have to change systems once you're in the tree. It's simple, safe, affordable and versatile. The drawbacks are it is slow and requires more upper body strength. But we are tree climbing here, so be prepared to break a sweat. Here is a step-by-step guide to setting up your split tail rope climbing system:

1. Clip the eyed end of the rope to your harness bridge with a locking carabinier.
2. Take your split tail and coil it around the other end of the rope at hip height.

Rope with eyed ends

Locking caribiner

Micro pulley

3. Put the micro pulley on the rope directly under the split tail.
4. Insert the locking carabiner through the top eye of the split tail, then both eyes of the pulley, then the bottom eye of the split tail.
5. Clip that same carabiner to your harness bridge directly next to your first carabiner.

You now have created a friction device that will allow you to move to almost every corner of the tree. Once you are practiced using this system it's actually pretty amazing the kind of swings and leaps you can safely make to get around. This works because if you weight the system, the

TOP LEFT *Coil your split tail around the other end of the rope at hip height.*
ABOVE *Insert the locking carabiner through the top eye of the split tail, then both eyes of the pulley, then the bottom eye of the split tail.*
BOTTOM LEFT *Clip that same carabiner to your harness bridge directly next to your first carabiner.*

Foot locking allows you to stand up on the rope by wrapping the rope around your foot

split tail bites the rope and won't let you move down. But if you pull up on the slack end of the rope, the split tail lets go and you can take in slack. The split tail is a friction hitch, meaning that like a seat belt, it can move slowly, but if pulled on hard it will lock up. Now that you have set up your system, test it by taking in slack and sitting down. You will have to sit down fast the first time to get the split tail seated properly. If you set it up properly, you will now be weighting your harness fully. If not, you will be sitting on the ground.

The split tail is a tool that keeps track of your upward progress, but your body is what moves you upward. To do this you use a technique called foot locking. Remember in elementary school gym class when you climbed the rope? If you knew foot locking then you would have been an all star. Foot locking is simply a way to wrap the rope around your foot so that you can step on the rope and stand up.

Once you stand up, take in slack on your split tail and sit back down. You are now two feet higher on the rope and so begins the upward

The split tail system keeps track of your upward progress as you use foot locking to move up the rope.

journey. Grab above your split tail on the rope, set your foot lock, stand up, take in slack, sit down and repeat. From a distance you will look like an inchworm climbing the line.

Once you have ascended high enough to stand on the first branch, take a breather and begin to inspect the tree or set rigging lines. You can lean against your top rope to get almost any-where in the tree. You can even walk out to the tips of branches by dividing your weight between the rope and the branch. This system will keep you safe in the tree, but it is up to you to figure out how you like to move amongst the branches. You can also use your flipline to act as a second

attachment point to keep you from swinging if you are horizontally far away from your top rope. If at any point you want to move your top rope to a new crotch, you can clip yourself to the tree with the flipline, weight it, and undo your top rope. It's very important to not drop your rope when pulling it down. The golden rule: Any time you switch from one tie in to another, always weight your new system before you unclip your old system. To descend out of the tree, simply sit in your harness, put your hand on top of the split tail and push down. The pressure of your hand will break the friction hitch and you will slide down the rope. As a beginner, its best to wear a glove to avoid rope burn in case you get going too fast.

If you are going to be doing a lot of ascending into trees then I recommend getting an ascender. With a double rope ascender you can move upwards fast and with much less effort. To use this technique pull both ends of the rope to the ground and tie them off to a sling on the trunk of the tree. Leave six feet of slack on the ground. Assemble the ascender on the ropes as shown right.

Be sure to read the instructions that come with the ascender. At this point you can foot lock like before, but you will move faster because you will be moving up a fixed line as opposed to pulling rope through the system. When foot locking on a double rope system, wrap both ropes around the foot and step on it. Once you are in the tree, clip into a branch with your flipline and set up the split tail system.

Soft goods such as ropes and harnesses are extremely strong but can be compromised when exposed to excessive sunlight, freezing temperatures, solvents or abrasion. If you purchase a climbing product, carefully read the instructions. Even if you choose to work off of a ladder, setting up a top rope makes the process much easier and safer. You literally cannot fall. Not to mention you can swing from one end of the treehouse to another. This is useful if you have to take measurements or tack screws in to hold beams together without weighting the structure and knocking everything out of level.

A double rope ascender allows you to move upwards quickly and with much less effort.

pruning

Like climbing, working on a tree is a world unto itself. Bringing a chain saw into a tree is dangerous and should be done with extreme caution. It is, however, a necessary part of building treehouses. With that said, never hesitate to hire a reputable professional. You may find that the tree you want to build in has dead wood hanging above the build site. You may find that there is an unwanted branch in the way of your foundation beam. Sometimes you must preform a weight reduction in the crown in order to compensate for the extra weight you'll be adding with the house. There are hundreds of techniques used by arborists to prune trees so that they are healthier or better fit their surroundings. Because every tree species is different, there are no rules that apply to every pruning scenario. Once you identify the species of your tree, you will have to do some research to find out what specific pruning rules apply to that species. You can pre-form different styles of pruning to get different responses from the tree. You may prune to remove disease, stimulate growth, protect your house, reduce competition within the canopy, or change the shape of the tree for aesthetic reasons.

Generally, it's best to prune in late winter and early spring before the growing season starts. Certain trees are sensitive to wilt, insects, sun scald-ing and fungal diseases, which can be easily spread in the summer and fall months. You also want to avoid removing too much of the canopy from a tree. A general rule of thumb is to never remove more than 30 percent of a tree's foliage. I would recommend consulting with a professional if you are considering drastically changing your tree. I also would recommend avoiding pruning your tree altogether if you don't have to. If the tree's doing great and nothing is structurally wrong or in the way of your treehouse, then let nature do its thing. This chapter isn't focused as much on when and why to prune, but more on how to safely prune to protect yourself and your treehouse. Sometimes you absolutely have to prune before you build, and I want to make sure you have a general understanding of how to do that if you are on site and facing this task as your next step.

Make your initial cut a few feet away from where the branch meets the trunk. Create a snap-cut by first making a small cut on the bottom of the branch and then cutting from the top as shown. Finally, cut off the remainder of the branch to create a collar cut.

Here are a few rules to follow when using a chain saw in a tree:

1. Make sure your chain saw will not slip and hit your rope, lanyard or body.
2. Try to position yourself above the cut and away from the direction the branch will fall.
3. Use both your rope and your lanyard to stay tied into the tree (in case you cut through one of them on accident). Do this unless it is safer to swing away from the cut after the branch is released.
4. Always inspect what and who is below you before you start cutting.
5. Keep the bottom of your climbing rope free of branches as you work in case you need to come down quickly.
6. Work with a partner on the ground.
7. Work slowly, double check everything and trust your gut.

When you decide to prune your tree, make a plan before you enter the tree. You often cannot tell what exactly you'll need to do once you're up in the tree. It's also best to always have someone on the ground as a second set of eyes, rope man, and someone to help in case of emergency. To make a cut on a branch to encourage compartmentalization of the wound (trees block off wounds to the rest off the tree; they do not heal and create new living tissue), first cut the branch a few feet away from where it grows off of the trunk. Make a small cut on the bottom of the branch, about a quarter of the way through the branch. Then come to the top of the branch and move an inch forward (towards the tip of the branch) and begin to cut the branch off. The bottom incision prevents the branch from peeling and creates a snap-cut that makes the branch pop off and fall parallel to the earth. Now that you have an unweighted stub, move back to the collar of the branch and make a cut down the center of the collar slightly sloping away from the trunk at an angle. Do not cut the branch off flush with the trunk, and do not leave extra branch that will just die and eventually fall off. This technique provides the easiest wound for the tree to close. View the images above for a visual demonstration of the collar cut.

If you cannot let the branch drop for whatever reason – for example, it's hanging over other branches you want to keep or over a structure – then you can set up a rope and pulley to lower the branch in a controlled manner.

Again, this is a scenario with many ways to complete the task. Creativity, common sense and

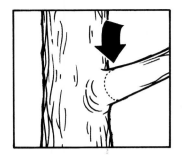
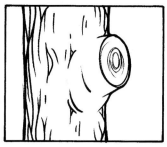
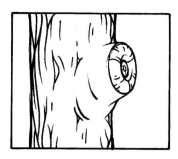

The collar cut promotes compartmentalization of the wound.

Use a rope and pulley to lower branches when you cannot safely allow them to drop.

good judgment are all needed to rig branches down safely. The illustration on page 37 shows a very simple version of how it could look. Tie the branch off using a running bowline. Tie it a few feet in front of your cut so that the tips of the branch will outweigh the butt. If the butt is heavier, the tips could come back at you and result in injury. Run the rope to a pulley on a sling that you have placed on a branch higher in the tree. In a pinch you can simply run the rope through a crotch higher up in the tree. Make sure your rigging anchor point is strong enough to hold the branch you are cutting. Then have your friend on the ground hold the rope (with gloves on). Use good communication, and when you begin the top cut of the branch, your friend can brace themselves for taking the weight of the wood. It is best if your friend lowers the branch immediately. If they hold the rope taught, the branch will stay at the same height as you and could swing back in and hit you. If the piece of tree is heavier than your friend can hold, then you can use friction to make it easier. One way to do this is to use a port-a-wrap, which is a device designed for this specific purpose. The port-a-wrap allows you to add friction to the rope and make one person strong enough to hold hundreds of pounds. The photo at right is an example of how to use a port-a-wrap.

The left rope goes to the hands of the ground guy while the right rope goes into the tree and holds up the branch being worked on. The heavier the branch, the more wraps you put around the port-a-wrap. This allows precision control while lowering the branch out of the tree.

A port-a-wrap allows you to add friction to the rope and increases your ability to hold heavier branches.

If you don't have a port-a-wrap, you can create friction off of the tree. A simple way to do this is to have your friend on the ground stand so that the rope wraps slightly around the trunk of the tree. The bigger the branch, the more surface of the rope should be touching the trunk. You never want to have so much friction that the branch won't come down because that could result in a heavy piece of wood swinging around near the climber. If a big piece of wood pins a climber into the trunk, it could result in serious injury or death.

tools of the trade

Throughout this book I will mention tools that are really handy to have on site and what tasks you might need them for. I will explain their uses in further detail later, but in efforts to help you put together your own set of tools without flipping through the pages, I have listed them here as a reference.

High powered drill for boring into trees
I prefer the Milwaukee Hole-Hawg because the shape of it allows you to get right behind the bit and apply pressure. This is easier with any drill on the ground, but if you're balanced on a ladder or hanging from a harness the right drill can save a lot of energy.

3" speed borer and a set of auger bits
You will need these bits to install treehouse attachment bolts (TABs), lag bolts and eye bolts. Spade bits may drill more quickly, but they can wander a lot more than an auger bit. Make sure you measure the diameter of your tree before you purchase bits. If your bit isn't long enough to go all the way through (if you are through-bolting), it's not worth the risk of trying to align the hole from the other side of the trunk. Also remember: Sharp bits are better for the tree's health.

Battery powered tool set
Having a nice battery powered circular saw and impact driver at the very least can save your shoulders when making those hard to reach adjustments while hanging in a harness. A corded set can definitely get the job done, but once you experience the agility of a cordless set, it all seems worth the cost.

Tree-climbing gear
Tree-climbing gear should include a harness, a helmet, tree-climbing ropes, a throw line, a flipline or lanyard, a spliced split tail, a micro pulley and two locking carabiners. For full descriptions check out the tree-climbing gear list in the chapter three.

High powered drill

3" speed borer

Auger bits

HEAVY DUTY
HOLE HAWG
Milwaukee

Locking carabiner

Helmet

Locking carabiner

Double rope ascender

Throw line

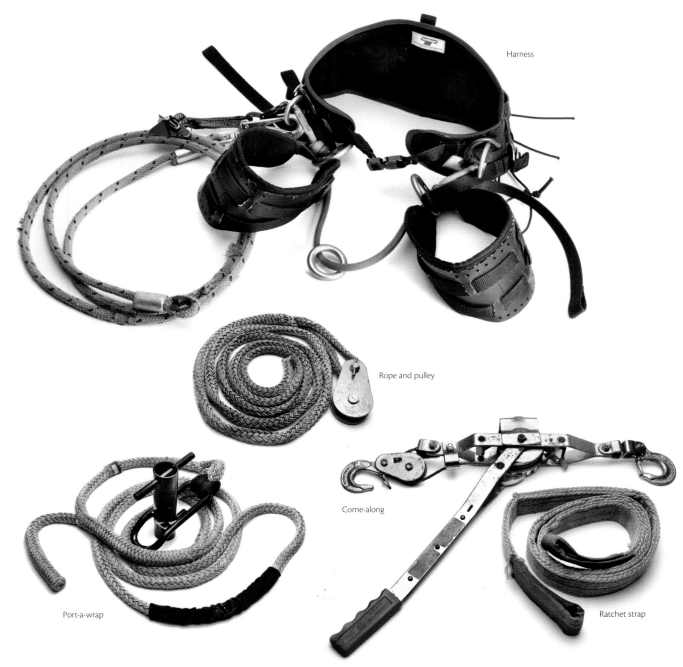

Harness

Rope and pulley

Come-along

Port-a-wrap

Ratchet strap

Rigging equipment

Strong ropes and pulleys will allow you to hoist beams or even pre-assembled structures into the trees with ease. Check out chapter eight on rigging to see a complete list of rigging tools and where to buy them.

Towing straps and webbing slings

You can never have enough slings to wrap around the tree to move things. They are so handy and can get you out of a lot of jams. Buy the beefy ones; a solid 2" webbing with sewn eyes at the end will do the trick. Get multiples and of varying lengths. Check the load limit on the tag when you buy it. If there isn't a load limit, don't make the purchase. Over the years I have leaned toward getting the strongest ones I can find, simply for peace of mind.

Ratchet straps and come-alongs

Throw a sling around the tree, a sling around your deck, and a come-along between the two and effortlessly move your treehouse to get it to sit where you need it to while you add fasteners. Use 2" ratchet straps to lock beams into place or move smaller loads. You can use them to lift a corner of your structure to get it level, or use them corner to corner to make it square.

Water level

Finding level in an organic environment can be tricky; a water level is without a doubt the best way to do so. It is simply a clear plastic tube filled mostly with water, but provides a tried and true technique that is reliable in an organic setting. Essentially the two ends of the tube can be raised to find a level measurement of height between two points – once the water line in each end of the tube settles, you have found level. See chapter nine for a full explanation of how to use this tool.

Generator

You will need a generator to power your tree boring drill if you can't reach power.

Chain saw

A chain saw is handy not only for pruning, but for making quick rough cuts while framing.

Spud bar

Having a lot of leverage comes in handy.

Pipe wrench with cheater bar

You will use this to tighten the TAB bolts and lag bolts into the trees.

Magnetic torpedo level

You will need this to ensure you're drilling level into the trees.

Water level

Blowtorch
This will quickly sanitize your tools before using them to penetrate the tree.

Standard framing tool set
This includes all of your normal framing tools such as a speed square, tape measurer, 4-foot level, hammers, tool belt, saws and drills.

Of course with all power tools you should exercise extreme caution. The reality is that if you take a power tool and add hanging in a harness to the equation, it multiplies the risk. It is important to use caution, especially if you are not used to working off of the ground. When it comes to rigging, you want to be extremely careful if someone is positioned under a heavy object while it is being raised. Make sure your rigging setup is rated to lift the loads you are attempting. Misuse of rigging gear can result in serious injury.

ASSEMBLING YOUR TEAM
If you're planning to put together a crew for your build, try to rally folks with strengths in areas where you are weak. Having someone who can manage the rigging while you think about the framing and someone else runs the ground crew will expedite your process. And sharing the workload is always nice. When it comes to working in the trees, there is no better help than a climber because you want someone who can move around the treetops with speed and agility (if I could hire monkeys to help me, I would). If you have access to a climbing community – be it tree, rock or utility – seek them out and find out what they have to offer.

attaching to the tree

Now that your tree is selected, prepped and ready for a treehouse, it is time to design and plan your build. The first step to designing your treehouse is figuring out where and how to attach to the tree. The way you attach to your tree is the most important decision you will make about your treehouse. This decision must be well thought out. You must take the trees' anatomy and health into extreme consideration. What makes treehouse building challenging and fun is that you have to create a structure that will be load bearing, that can move, and that will come into contact with its foundation (the trees) as little as possible. Here are the golden rules of treehouse attachment. (We will discuss details on how to follow these rules later on in the book.)

1. Trees are vascular beings. The outer layer of a tree is called the cambium. This is where nutrients flow throughout the tree. If you constrict the cambium, you will strangle the tree and kill it. If you poke too many holes in the cambium, nutrient flow will not be able to make upward progress, and you could kill the tree. The best way to attach to the tree is to maximize use of the structural heartwood (center dead wood of the tree) and minimize penetration of the cambium. This means that your treehouse should be held up by a few very strong points of contact with the tree.

2. Trees grow. As a tree gets older, it will grow upward from the top, and outward from the trunk. It is a myth that a tree that has grown around a fence will lift the fence into the air. If you put a nail in a tree at head height, 40 years later, that nail will still be at head height; although it will be inside the tree now. Trees can grow very fast outward. Each growing season they add another ring, which means that the tree will get thicker and thicker as time goes on. You have to frame your treehouse in a way that allows for tree growth. If you can't build far off of the tree, then you have to frame and deck in a way that can be changed to allow for a bigger tree down the line.

3. Trees move. If you build in one tree, the treehouse can sway with the tree as the wind blows. However, if you build in multiple trees, you must use dynamic attachment points so that the treehouse doesn't fight with the moving tree. I assure you that a windstorm can provide enough force to rip screws right out of your structure. The higher you are in the tree, the more you have to account for movement and the more dynamic your attachment point must become.

When building in multiple trees, you have to approach the attachment points as a physics puzzle. When the wind blows, each individual tree will move in its own way unrelated to its neighbors. If you don't allow for enough movement, you can risk stressing your hardware. If you allow for too much movement, you can end up with a treehouse that gives you motion sickness. Trees can actually benefit from a treehouse because the structure can add support and keep the tree from reaching excessive wind loads. In an urban environment, you will see people cable their tree crotches to prevent large limbs from snapping out. Cables hold trees together in a big windstorm and, depending on your treehouse design, your platform could do the same. Because I am not a master craftsman, I like to design structures that are adjustable. This way, if I don't get things perfectly level or square the first time, I can go back and tweak things to sit how I want them to. I will explain these techniques by examples in chapter nine.

The type of attachment you choose will be largely determined by how high you build. If you are attaching to a tree that plays a big role in holding your treehouse up, you want the diameter of the trunk where you are attaching to be no less than 12". You can get away with a smaller diameter if the tree isn't holding that much weight, or if you are building a really small treehouse in a really small tree. There is a sliding scale to follow when deciding on attachment methods. The lower you are to the ground, and the thicker the trunk is, the more rigid your hardware can be. The higher you are, the more dynamic your hardware should be.

If you are building in one tree, you can use fixed hardware as long as you still account for tree growth. One tree will still move in the wind, but it won't fight with another tree. Your treehouse will simply move with it wherever it goes. As soon as you add a second or third tree you must include dynamic hardware into the equation.

If you are building on a really large trunk at a height of six feet or lower, you probably do not need a dynamic attachment point. Use common sense: Does the trunk look like it can move much at the height you are building? If you are between six and thirty-five feet, you can most likely use hardware such as the treehouse attachment bolt (TAB) coupled with a sliding bracket. If you are above thirty-five feet, a suspended load system, such as cable, will work best for holding your treehouse up. Of course, these numbers are loose guidelines. The tree type and thickness of the trunk will also be factors when deciding what kind of attachment to use. If you want to be really sure, go to your build site on a windy day and observe the movement of your host trees. You can even climb them in the wind if you want! Here are some guidelines to follow when designing the structural platform of your treehouse.

- Trees almost always move more than you expect, not less.
- It is better to have to add rigidity to a structure, than to take it away.

Special care should be used when drilling the hole for the treehouse attachment bolt (TAB). Be sure that you are ready to drill into the tree and take measures to sanitize your tools and equipment.

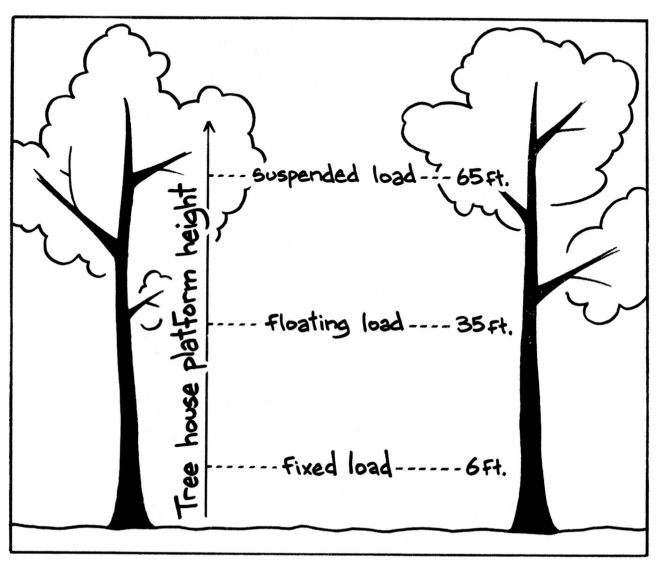

Different types of attachment are recommended for different platform heights.

- Plan several designs for your treehouse using multiple kinds of hardware and weigh the pros and cons.
- There is almost always a better design and hashing out the physics with friends is an exciting phase before building.

When I was drawing the structural design for the treehouse featured in this book, I had over ten different versions. All of them would have worked, but some had more points of contact with the tree, some of them were not adjustable, and some of them would be fine but were just plain boring. In the end I went with the design I knew would be strong, adjustable, have minimal points of entry into the cambium, and look good.

There are different types of hardware for attaching to trees. The TAB, or treehouse attachment bolt, is a specialized piece of hardware designed to hold large loads in a tree, while minimizing impact on the cambium and consolidating compartmentalization. There are different sizes depending on how big your treehouse is and there are different kinds of brackets you can use on the TAB depending on what kind of structure and movement you desire. For smaller treehouses with fixed loads, you can use a large lag bolt. For suspended loads you can use galvanized aircraft cable to hang the treehouse.

The different kinds of attachment can be referred to as fixed, floating or suspended. Below are explanations of each method.

Fixed: A fixed structure should be used when dealing with one tree. If you have two trees you can also make one tree fixed and the other dynamic. A fixed attachment is the easiest to work with because it is the most similar to typical construction. One thing to keep in mind is that although this point doesn't have to move, the tree will still grow; that's why when using fixed brackets you build with the bracket slid far out on the bolt allowing space between the bracket and the tree.

Floating: This method is probably the most used and most comfortable style of attachment. The floating bracket goes on the TAB, and can slide in any direction except up or down. These are great because they allow for movement but don't have the bouncy feeling you get when hanging on a cable. Whenever you have a sliding bracket it is crucial to remember while framing that the bracket can move back toward the tree. You wouldn't want any of your woodwork to make contact with the tree before the bracket bottoms out on the TAB. Otherwise your framing or decking will scar the cambium.

Suspended: Hanging a treehouse from cables is structurally sound, extremely dynamic for tree movement, and endlessly adjustable. I love working with cable for these reasons. I think it's one of the best ways to build a treehouse at high elevation in multiple trees. The downside of cable is that if your load isn't thought out properly you can create a giant swing that moves with every step. Whenever you build with cable, use a turnbuckle to make it easily adjustable.

COMMON MISTAKES

Once I developed a keen eye for treehouses, I started seeing them in backyards whenever I was driving. I often climb into a tree for pruning and find remnants of some kid's forgotten tree fort. Occasionally I get so curious I have to knock on a family's front door and ask questions about their design. Because of this, I get to see how different trees have reacted to treehouses over time.

Bolting a large beam directly to the trunk can choke a tree to death.

I also get to discover treehouse flaws and learn what ultimately led to their demise. I have also made plenty of mistakes on my own and had to go back and correct them if possible. Obviously, the more you think through possible flaws and eliminate them, the longer your treehouse will go without needing repair or removal. Make an effort to avoid mistakes made by other builders by studying treehouses that you encounter. Look for ways they could be better. Here is a list of common mistakes many builders make.

1. **Building a rigid structure.** Trees are going to move, period. The wind blows and nails pull. Everything comes apart and out of the tree.

2. **Setting boards in crotches of trees.** This weakens the crotch. This can also cut off nutrient flow and harm the tree. Plus, water can collect in the crotch and that will speed up decay of the lumber.

3. **Bolting a large beam directly to the trunk.** This can choke a tree to death because as the tree grows wider the cambium is pinched as it grows around the board. This can also happen over time if your treehouse frame too close to the trunk.

4. **Overly ambitious designs.** Weaving branches through the room of the treehouse looks awesome and can be done successfully. A lot of thought has to be put into where the framing is and how the tree will move. More often than not, the tree beats the treehouse from the inside out. Capturing this aesthetic is most easily done with just a few bigger branches low to their previous scaffold (remember, a twig comes from a branch, which comes from a bough, which comes from a trunk).

5. **Poking too many holes into a tree.** It may be comforting to see the additional bolt or series of screws, but placing too many holes in a tree can disrupt nutrient flow and kill it. You have to be especially thoughtful when the holes are close

together on a tree. I like to try to spread out the impact and let each wound compartmentalize. If you have to have multiple points of contact with the cambium that need to be close together, do not stack them vertically. This can cause the wood between the holes to lose all circulation and die.

6. **Building your treehouse to be too dangerous for use.** This may sound obvious, but I have surprisingly seen this so often. Rickety old lumber nailed way up in a tree with a 2x4 ladder leading a slanted way to the top is an accident waiting to happen. I am all for hanging out in the very tops of trees, but if you put yourself or your friends in that kind of position, make sure you have total confidence in your design!

7. **Building a treehouse that is too big for its host.** This can lead to having to install ground posts or even to tree failure. If you are unsure and want to do the math to find out what your trees can hold, calculate the weight of your structure, and look up a wood load calculator online. You can type in your tree species and dimensions of the trunk and get a rough idea of what kind of stresses that wood type can withstand.

Always err on the side of caution. You never want to push a tree to its limits.

ETHICS

Ethics are opinions. I hold the Canopy Crew and myself to a high standard when it comes to treatment of the tree and purity of design. Treehouses are different and special. You are making a bond with a living being that could be literally holding your life in its boughs. I believe that keeping the tree in your mind as something that deserves special treatment once you start building is necessary. I also think that there is a difference between a house built around trees and a house built in the trees. Sometimes, a post down to the ground is absolutely needed to make your treehouse dream a reality, and that's absolutely fine. Sometimes you have a design flaw and you have to go back and add a leg to keep things standing. But if you want to harness the magic of a pure treehouse, you should keep the legs off of the ground, and feel what it is like to float through the canopy. Design your structure around this concept. The wind will blow and all of your neighbors will begin to slowly sway back and forth. It is not unlike the open sea when your sails catch new wind. There is something undeniably healing and humbling about it. Above all, respect the trees.

BUILDING YOUR TREEHOUSE

treehouse design

You now have a basic understanding of how to select a tree, move about in a tree and prep your build site. You are prepared with the necessary tools to get the job done efficiently.

It is time to put the pencil to paper and hash out various designs for your treehouse. It's good to keep an open mind when designing. I like to start with my desired aesthetic. What is the dreamiest treehouse I can think of? Then I will work backwards from there. Usually this means trimming off the excess to get to a realistic design that works with my trees and budget. Once you have selected the trees you will build in, follow these steps to eventually find your final design.

1. Measure each tree's diameter and the distance between the trees themselves. Sketch this roughly to scale and label each tree so you know the orientation.

2. Start by running through a few different beam configurations. The beams will hold the platform, which will hold the treehouse. Where does the weight sit on the beams? Where does the treehouse need to be the strongest and where will it be the lightest?

   You can attach the structure to a particular group of trees using several different means. Keep this in mind – especially if you are still deciding between using TABs or cables to hold up the platform.

3. Take your top three favorite beam layouts and figure out several different ways you could attach them to the trees. How will the trees move and grow in relation to the beams? How high do you want to build and what style of attachment do you need to accommodate tree movement at this height? Think of several different ways that could work – even if you know some of them aren't ideal. A unique perspective could lead to the best design.

4. Think about your attachment methods. A beautiful cabin in the trees isn't worth much if it's mounted poorly. If you are not sure you are skilled enough to design a balanced hanging treehouse, choose

Your initial sketches should account for tree diameter and distance between trees.

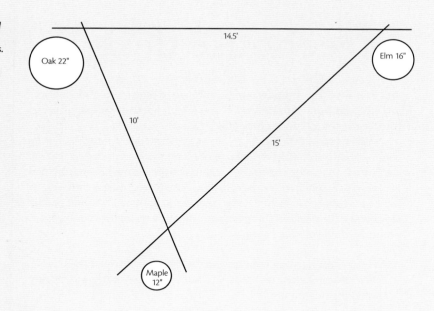

Oak 22"

14.5'

Elm 16"

10'

15'

Maple 12"

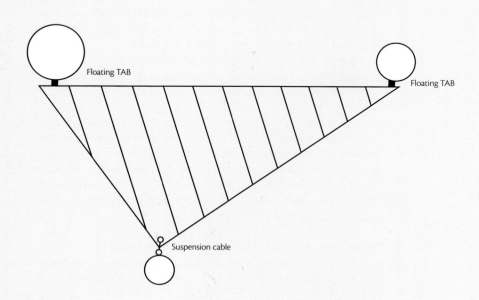

Floating TAB

Floating TAB

Suspension cable

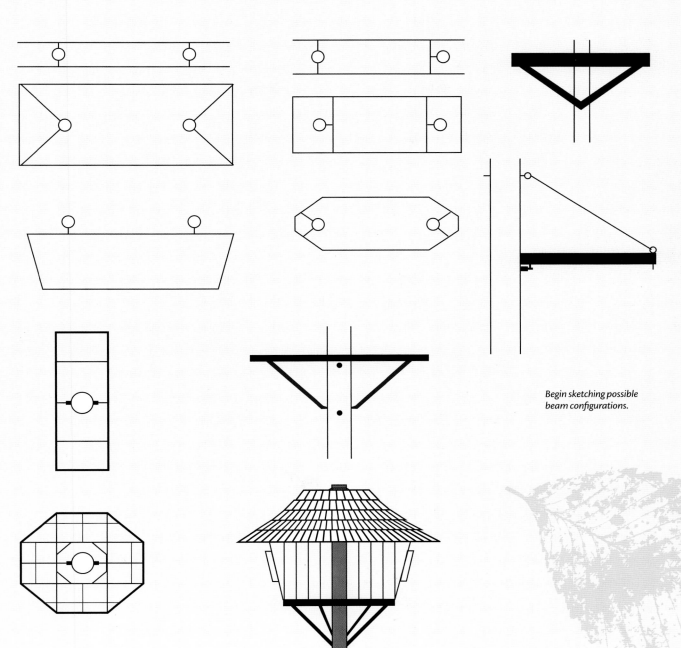

Begin sketching possible beam configurations.

a design that can't tip to one side or the other. You can also incorporate adjustable systems into your design such as turnbuckles. Think about it first from a structural stand point: Will these attachments be strong enough? Then think about it from the tree's standpoint: How will the holes in the bark affect nutrient flow? Are you placing too many holes close together?

5. Scan your design for flaws. The more time you spend thinking about all of the ways your treehouse could be flawed, the better treehouse designer you will become. Think about how the trees will move in relation to the treehouse in a storm. How much space do you have between the beams and the trunk? Will the trees be in the way of your living area?

6. Work with what you have. If you have small trees, then design with weight in mind. If you have big spans between trees, then focus on making sure that your foundation beam can withstand that long stretch. Conform your treehouse to its trees and you will be setting your house up for a long life.

7. After weighing the pros and cons of your best designs, select the option that best fits your trees. Some readers will have different needs from a treehouse than others. If you are building a treehouse for little kids, you probably don't need it to live a long life as the tree grows bigger. Designing a treehouse with plans to take it down when the tree outgrows it may make sense for your lifestyle or budget. If you are building a treehouse for adults, you should keep the tree's longevity at the forefront of your design.

I build treehouses in stages. Thinking about everything at once can be overwhelming. First I build the platform, which will hold the house up. This is usually the hardest part, or the most unfamiliar part. Then I will build the house that sits on top. For more eccentric architecture, this isn't always possible. If you choose to build in stages, make sure your design time overlaps. You don't want to build a platform that will last 40 years and put on a roof that will cut into the bark in five years. Keep searching for flaws as you design and build. You will almost always have to make sacrifices in your design in order to keep the trees happy.

When your supports are trees, you have to work with them with regard to spacing. You are often faced with large spans and long cantilevers. Make sure that the beams you are using can withstand the applied loads. Also remember that these guidelines change depending on the diameter of the trunk and how high you are in the tree. The best thing to do is get to know your trees specifically. Find out how they move and imagine how a treehouse would react to that. While a gentle 1" sway might not look like much to the naked eye, it's enough to pull a screw out. If you're building in a single tree you don't have to worry about movement in the same way. That tree can sway and carry the treehouse with it. It won't be fighting another tree or playing tug-a-war with your structure.

For me doing quick rough sketches is the most effective way to work out the kinks. If I spend time on concept sketches I get attached

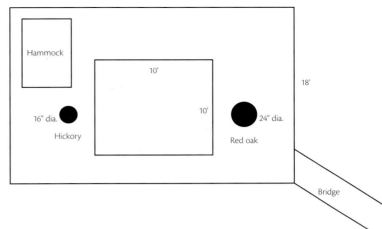

to designs and details that may not be the top choice. Think about who will be using the tree-house: That will change little details, like head room and the size of the interior space.

I also try to keep the surrounding environment in mind when designing the treehouse. Ample deck space for canopy viewing is a must for me. I want to be able to feel cozy and nested, but I also want to feel the exposure and height of being up in a tree. I want to feel like I'm still outside when it's raining, even though I am sheltered and dry. Sometimes it makes more sense to build in simpler trees that look out over the crown jewels of the forest. Building in the branches of a tree provides an amazing feel, but it is definitely harder to pull off than just attaching to the trunk. Consider your skill level as a carpenter when dreaming big.

I prefer using entrance methods that are unique or treehouse appropriate such as a swinging bridge or a rope ladder. Having an entrance like that makes your mindset change on the way into the treehouse. A rope ladder will engage your sense of play and encourages monkeying around. A rigid staircase can detract from the suspended feeling of being up in the trees.

When you source materials, make sure you aren't just going with what you know because it's easy. This can lead to poor scenarios. Plaster can crack, nails can pull, and asphalt roofs are heavy. I mean, who wants to put a bunch of rocks in the trees anyway? It just doesn't feel right. Do you want to create a ground house in the trees? Or do you want to create a house specifically tailored to its habitat?

The most common pitfall when designing a treehouse is underestimating tree movement and growth. It is not easy breaking rules you may have previously learned about construction. But with treehouses, more fasteners don't always equal a stronger house. Really think about where the house will sit in relation to the tree. Does the tree lean at all? If so, will it lean away or into the roof of the house? Sometimes you can accidentally design for a lot of movement in all directions except one. Take time to try to imagine all different movement scenarios. Take time to see if there is a design that requires less penetration of the bark. Remember that trees grow outward and upward from the top, but they don't grow upward from the trunk.

Perhaps you want to start with something easy. If you want to build the easiest treehouse possible, with the most bang for your buck, I would recommend a design that's between two trees that sits ten feet off of the ground. With two trees, you aren't building something that will teeter in the middle. It is easy to visualize and predict what's going to happen. At ten feet you can still work off of a ladder and won't need much rigging, but you are at least high enough where someone won't be able to reach up and touch it. There is nothing wrong with keeping it simple, safe and within your skill level.

Having an appropriate entrance such as a swinging bridge or a rope ladder can encourage a playful mindset and set the tone for time spent in your treehouse.

rigging

My first entry to rigging was through rock climbing. I learned mostly accidentally though problem solving while on the cliffs. It wasn't until I pursued my High Angle 3 rescue certification that I really dove into the technical details of setting up rigging systems. I had the opportunity to take the course with the guy who wrote the book, literally. The class, taught by instructor and author Rick Weber, was designed as a prep course for people who wanted to be involved in search and rescue – specifically in mountainous terrain where you would have to get an injured person off of a cliff. While these rigging scenarios were far more complex than what we generally use for treehouse building, the principals are the same. One thing is for certain: In-field experience is what makes you a good rigger.

For me, figuring out the rigging to get a treehouse into a tree is one of the best parts of design. Each scenario is a puzzle and you never really know how things will go until you start pulling on the ropes! It is important to remember that problem solving as you go is a normal part of rigging. Don't get discouraged when your beams swing to a completely different spot than you anticipated. This is just part of the puzzle and an opportunity to set up a new system to get things where you need them to be.

When dealing with large pieces of lumber, swinging through the trees, you have to remember to take it slow and be safe. Now is a great time to put on your helmet. Make sure the gear and ropes you have are rated as strong enough to move the loads you are attempting to move. If you don't have a ton of fancy gear in your system, then a lot of friends can do the trick.

My number one rule for designing your rigging setup is to keep it simple. A simple rigging sytem is generally easier to predict, adjust and use because there are fewer steps and moving parts to keep track of. If you are familiar with pulley systems then you can build more complex setups. Usually, a three-to-one pulley system, with a progress capture and tag line will do the trick for moving beams. Let's look at a few possibilities of what your system might look like.

A pulley system gives one person the strength of multiple people in exchange for pulling more rope through for upward progress. For example, a three-to-one pulley system gives one man the strength of three, but

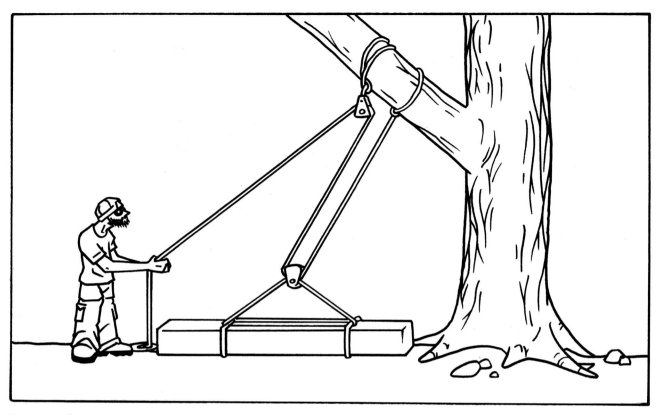

Two-to-one pulley system

three times the rope has to be pulled through the system to move the object upward one unit. You can build a pulley system that gives you the strength of two, three, four and so on.

Progress capture refers to a device or technique used that won't allow your beam to slide back down once you have raised it. There are mechanical devices such as a Grigri or port-a-wrap that can help you with this. However, in a pinch you can always just tie the rope off to a tree on the ground.

A tag line is a rope tied to the beam to control swing or movement as you raise it into the tree. It's important to think about how the beam will move and where the tag line will need to go in order to counteract that movement.

When preparing your system to lift treehouse parts into the trees, you first must look at what you are lifting. Usually treehouse lumber isn't insanely heavy because unless you are in a giant tree, you probably aren't building a giant treehouse. Say, for example, you have a beam that weighs 150 pounds: You need to raise this

Find your anchor point.

beam twenty feet into the air, level it, and set it onto a TAB bolt. While one strong person may be able to lift that beam, when you take into consideration friction and the need to hold it up and adjust its height for long periods of time, you realize that a good rigging system is needed. Below is a step-by-step example of how to set up a three-to-one system that would be appropriate for treehouse building.

Step 1: Find your anchor point
Your anchor point will be the highest point in your system and will generally take most of the weight and determine where the beam will hang. If you are attaching to the trunk, you can simply girth hitch a sling to the trunk of the tree and clip your first pulley to that sling. You can build your anchor off a higher branch as long as the beam won't swing out away from where you are attaching it. Believe it or not there is enough friction to hold that sling up while lifting the beam. I have lowered chunks of wood weighing 1,000 pounds off of one single sling, and they grip very well. It is important to note that ropes stretch. Make sure your anchor point is high enough above your TAB bolt (or attachment point), to raise the beam enough before your pulley system hits itself or bottoms out. For a three-to-one, you may need two anchor points.

Step 2: Gain mechanical advantage
Setting up a three-to-one is simple and the drawings will help you understand more than words will. Start by tying one end of the rope to the beam. Run the rope up through a pulley in the tree, back down to a pulley on the beam, back up to a second pulley in the tree, and then back down to the person hoisting. You can add more

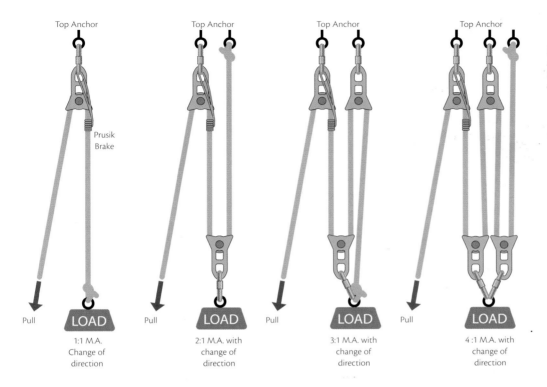

Prusik
Brake

Pull
LOAD
Pull
LOAD
Pull
LOAD
Pull
LOAD

1:1 M.A.
Change of
direction

2:1 M.A. with
change of
direction

3:1 M.A. with
change of
direction

4 :1 M.A. with
change of
direction

Four variations of pulley systems that can be used to create mechanical advantage.

pulleys to the equation, which will attain more lifting power, but it will also mean more rope will need to be pulled through the system. A three-to-one or five-to-one should get the job done. If you are venturing into nine-to-one territory, make sure you do the math because at that point you can actually create too much force and break parts of your system even with just one person pulling on the rope.

Step 3: Attaching to the beam
You can sling your beam just as you put a sling around the tree trunk. It is important to think about where the slings are in relation to the beam's weight. If you aren't balanced, then the

beam can tip vertically when raised, making it much more difficult to get into place. You can usually achieve balance by using two slings instead of one at either end of the beam. You can also set up a raising system on either end of your beam and lift each one a little bit at a time if you want to have more control over how your beam hangs.

Step 4: Progress capture
Progress capture refers to the ability to automatically keep the beam from lowering as you pull it up. There are many ways to do this and many fancy tools to make it effortless and smooth. In an effort to keep things simple, I will teach you a

handful of ways that utilize tools that are either cheap or are a worthwhile investment because of their wide variety of uses.

A. The simplest (and free) way to capture progress is to have one person pulling while a second takes the slack and bends it across the base of a tree. This provides a huge amount of friction and at any point the rope can be wrapped several times around the tree to lock off the system. One downside is that it can be a bit messy and your rope can tangle easily. You don't have as much control if you need to lower the beam.

B. You can use a friction hitch similar to a climbing split tail and a micro pulley to capture progress. I do not recommend mixing your climbing gear in with your rigging gear. What holds your life should never be forced to hold a heavy beam. A disadvantage is that a friction hitch can be very difficult to break and let slack out if loaded with a very heavy load.

C. A Grigri is a belay device designed to hold a human while rock climbing. While its not designed for rigging, it is handy because it allows rope to pass through but when pulled fast it bites down and holds the rope (similar to how a seat belt locks when you try to lean forward quickly). The Grigri also has a lever that allows you to lower the beam with extreme control. One downside is that you can't fit a large diameter rope into a Grigri.

D. A port-a-wrap is great because it is extremely strong, can take any diameter rope, can be used for lowering huge loads, and is extremely sensitive while lowering.

You can also use a port-a-wrap to lock off a beam while it is in the air.

Step 5: Tag line

A tag line is a second or third rope tied onto the beam and held on the ground to control swing or movement. For example, if you have a work station uphill of the trees you are building in, your beam may want to swing forward as you raise it off of the ground. You can use a tag line to slow the swing so you don't risk the beam smashing into the trunk. You can even apply friction to that rope using a tree trunk or a port-a-wrap to gain control over the lowering speed. When using a tag line, think about the direction of pull versus the angle of the line. Make sure the rope man isn't in a position to get pulled off of a ledge or down a hill.

Step 6: Redundancy

Redundancy is a concept strongly adhered to in rock climbing. If your life is hanging on a rope, always be attached to the rock with gear at least two times. This way, if one point breaks you won't fall to your death. While there are certainly times to apply this to rigging, it is not always needed. The reason you don't always want to is because more gear means more points to create friction or mistakes. Keeping it simple keeps progress moving along. If you are lifting a medium size load with gear that is rated for huge loads, and no one's life is on the line, then you don't need to double up every sling. If you are unsure of your system, or if you are pushing the limits of your gear, then, by all means, be redundant – add two slings at each connection point.

It is usually easiest to lift the beam higher than the attachment point, tie it off, regroup, and then lower it slowly into place. Having an extra set of hands is crucial. I like to have one person in the tree, above the whole operation, ready with screws and an impact driver to secure the beam. One or two people should be on the ropes lifting the weight of the beam and operating progress capture, and one person is a free hand to adjust the system or grab the rope if more strength is needed.

My technical ropework mentor Rick Weber, who taught the high angle rescue course I took, chimed in to remember a treehouse he built with his wife years ago.

"My wife, Liz, and I built only one treehouse in our lives. Located 52 feet off the ground in a giant beech tree supported on thick branches, it was an interesting challenge. To get building materials up there, we rigged a top pulley about four feet above the platform floor on a steel post secured to the trunk. We tied a rope to the material to be hoisted from the ground and ran it up and over the top pulley and back to the ground. Here the rope ran through another pulley connected via a tubular webbing anchor on the base of the tree and out to a golf cart, to which it was secured to the tow hitch. Also located on the webbing anchor at the base of the trunk was a Petzl shunt, which acted as a fail-safe brake in the event that the rope and/or the golf cart failed. If the rope broke, the load would remain stationary instead of falling.

This worked well for our project and didn't require any pulley systems to create mechanical advantage as the golf cart had plenty of power to pull the loads. For those not having a vehicle for a power source, pulley systems can be easily created to hoist heavier loads than could normally be done with just pulling up on a rope tied to the loads. The illustration on page 69 shows a simple change of direction rope system and three different systems for hoisting loads from the ground. These systems can be created with simple pulleys or double sheave pulleys. In essence these represent what is commonly referred to as block-and-tackle systems.

A two-to-one system will allow a person to hoist a load twice the weight that he can pull on the rope. A three-to-one system allows a person to hoist a load three times the force he can exert, and a four-to-one system allows a person to hoist a load four times the force he can exert.

Obviously, the load limitations meant we couldn't do a lot of preassembly on the ground, so much of the work was done above. Lumber was attached to the rope by drilling holes in non-stress-critical locations, threading the rope through and tying it off. Small materials and tools were raised in 5-gallon buckets. When rigging a pulley system to hoist materials up to a construction site in a tree, there are some common sense guidelines:

1. Don't hoist heavy loads. Anything over 400 pounds would make me nervous.
2. No one should be in the drop zone when a load is being hoisted.
3. Use a good quality rope. A new NFPA-rated static rope would be ideal, but it is quite expensive. A much cheaper alternative would be to use a retired dynamic climbing rope. If it hasn't been left out for long periods in the sun or subjected to chemicals, it should be able to hoist 400 pounds – a reasonable safety margin.
4. Use good quality pulleys. Again, new NFPA-rated pulleys would be ideal, but they are expensive. Try to find pulleys with strength ratings stamped on them and ones with sheaves no smaller than 2" in diameter.
5. Be sure your hoisting system includes a brake – such as a Prusik loop or Petzl shunt – to stop the load from falling in the event of a failure at the pulling end of the system.

Have one or more persons pulling the rope from the ground and one or more persons, safely tethered, aloft to receive the load.

—Rick Weber, retired mechanical engineer and author of many technical publications

When using rigging equipment, it is important to use the ropes and tools within their limits. If you are unsure of the gear's strength or how to use it, take time to educate yourself to avoid disaster. I learned this the hard way when raising a large prebuilt triangular platform into a three-tree treehouse early on in my career. I had a three-to-one pulley system set up on each tree with a progress capture on each system. We were going around to each tree raising the corners a few feet at a time. The system worked great except I used 1" webbing slings that I had cut and tied on my own. In theory, everything should have been fine. The webbing was rated to be strong enough, and there is nothing inherently wrong with making your own slings. The problem came from the knots. One-inch tubular webbing is rated for around 4,200 pounds. When you add a knot, its tensile strength is reduced to about 70 percent, or about 2,900 pounds. Then you add my body weight climbing up onto the platform and moving around. Such movement creates an impulse or shock load that can create a force several times the static load. With me on the platform the structure only statically weighed around 1,000 pounds. It is possible that the webbing had sustained UV damage from being used in the sun, or it could have simply been the case that I was bouncing the load too much. Ultimately one of the slings snapped and the whole side of the platform fell down about 15 feet. It all happened extremely fast and to this day I am amazed that I somehow jumped onto the tree trunk and remained unharmed.

The moral of the story is, over-engineer your rigging. Webbing and rope are fairly inexpensive. Buy a product that you know is strong enough. If there is any high-risk scenario, be redundant with your system and wear a harness to ensure nothing can go wrong.

While rigging is a great way to get lumber into trees, it is not always necessary. Ladders, scaffolds and brute strength have been getting the job done on your average construction site for years. Judge your build site and treehouse for yourself. Perhaps it makes the most sense to lift small beams into place by hand. Maybe building a scaffold around the tree is the fastest and easiest way to build. Sometimes building sections on the ground and passing them up preassembled greatly reduces build time. I am used to building on steep, dense terrain, where getting out of the thick of the forest floor is desired. Like I said earlier, ropework is my strength. Getting materials up into the trees is the fastest way for me to see progress. That isn't the case for every build site. If you are used to building in a specific style, try to stick to that style as much as possible so you feel at home and move quickly. If you are building a small treehouse, chances are you won't need to set up any rigging systems. If you have a small deck and the option to frame walls out on the ground and then raise them into the tree, then this is likely your easiest route.

the build

As much as researching and reading about treehouses helps, nothing hones your skills like doing the manual labor. I am always learning little tricks that make each step a little easier. This chapter is full of those pro tips that will let you skip all of the small obstacles along the way. I discuss each step of treehouse building in chronological order. I approach a challenging new build just like I would a big wall climb: I plan out the big picture ahead of time, but once I get started, I take it one day at a time. If I think about everything all at once it is easy to get overwhelmed and discouraged. Treehouse projects often feel overly ambitious at first. Don't let the entire build weigh you down; break it up into workdays. Day one might be prep and material staging. Day two could be TAB installs and any other tree drilling you will need. Day three would then be beam raising. I always account for a few hiccups along the way and add additional time in my estimate for the build.

Preparing for TAB install
When you are preparing to drill into the tree for the first time, take a long moment to acknowledge that you are about to pass the point of no return. Penetrating the cambium will forever alter that tree's biology. Do not rush this step or take it lightly. Make sure that your TAB placements are exactly where you want them. Climb the tree using a rope, ladder or both. The more stability you have, the better – especially when you're drilling into a hardwood. Position your body to have maximum leverage and use your lanyard around the tree to help keep you there. If you have multiple trees, you will need at least one other person in the other tree to help you find level.

I always use a water level. It is a tried and true technique that is reliable in an organic setting. String levels work, but aren't nearly as accurate. Laser levels can be great but are often times too hard to see on a sunny day. A water level is simply a clear plastic tube filled mostly with water. Put one person at the base of each tree and place your thumb on the top of the tube. This way, if one person climbs quicker than the other, the water won't spill out of the tube. If you don't have a ladder, have each climber carry up a string so they can pull the tube up simultaneously once they are in

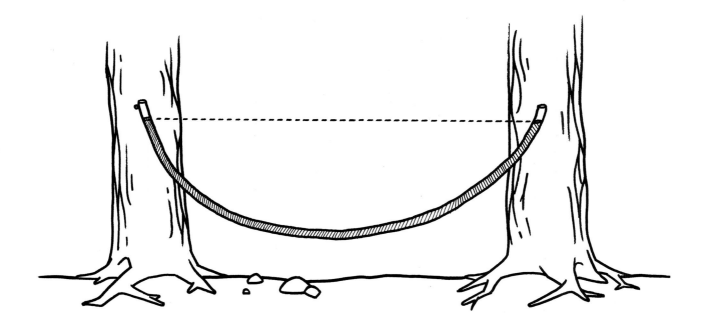

A water level is a tried and true technique for finding level that is reliable in an organic setting.

place. Person A should place the tube of water against the tree at the height off of the ground they want the bolt to sit. Person B can then use the line where the water sits in the tube to get a close idea of where person A is on the other tree. It takes several seconds, but if both people are still, the water line will cease to bob up and down and you will have perfect level. Both surfaces of the water on either end of the tube will be sitting level with each other. Take a thick sharpie and mark a line on both trees.

Now you have level and need to find the center of the trunk and a straight line between the two trees. Place a string around both trunks and pull it tight. Tie the string so it creates a loop around the two trees. If you have more than two trees, just repeat this process and double check your results from each tree to its neighbor. The

Place your TAB where there is the thickest section of heart wood.

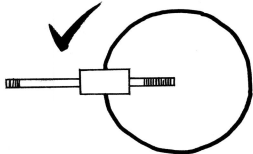

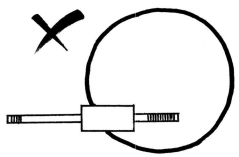

string will give you two straight lines that will act as a guide to show you how to point your drill bit. Depending on your design, you will want your bit to be parallel, perpendicular or at a certain angle to the string. Take a second shorter piece of string and place it against the trunk from one string to the other. If you take that distance and fold the string in half you will find the center of the trunk in relation to the direction you want your bolt to sit. Once you feel confident about your placement make an X with your marker or place a screw exactly where you want to drill. The purpose of this is to find the rough center of the trunk. As shown in the image above, you want to place the TAB where there is the thickest section of heartwood, not off to the side.

Take another moment to review your layout. Have a second set of eyes review it as well. Take a look from several angles. Do your lines look correct to match your plans? Double check level on all planes. Remember, once you drill, you are changing the tree forever. One thing that makes building in trees difficult is that your eyes might assume the trunks are straight when in reality they often grow with a lean. That combined with the slope of the ground can result in a lot of optical illusions. Time after time I have looked

I sanitize all of my drill bits and hardware right before entering the tree and between each tree. This protects the trees from fungus or bacteria being spread. Not all trees are susceptible to disease transfer this way, but I don't like to take any chances. Keep a small blowtorch handy and go over the surfaces of your bits. You don't have to roast them; just leave the flame on long enough to sanitize.

at a treehouse and thought it was severely out of level, but when I checked, everything was fine.

Once you have triple checked your layout, you'll have your first hole marked and are ready to drill. I view this stage as if I was a surgeon. Measure three or four times before drilling. You only have one shot to get it perfect. Messing up could result in tree damage and could mean you have to think of a new design to make up for your mistake. I start with my first TAB and measure off of it for each tree after that.

Drilling the TAB hole

After you have your hole marked, look at the TAB you purchased and measure the different parts. There are different sized TABs for different sized treehouses and trees. I generally use the largest TAB if my treehouse is bigger than one hundred square feet and if my tree size allows it. That size isn't going off anything other than my personal opinion. I would rather have too much strength than not enough. The larger TABs also allow for more tree growth, which means more time before you would ever have to consider altering anything. The TAB consists of a tiered bolt with different sized parts. The threads enter the tree fully, the collar or boss (3" section) enters the tree half way (depending on size of TAB), and the stem or perch (unthreaded section) sticks out from the tree and holds your beam. Depending on which TAB you buy, you will need to drill different depth holes.

To drill for the TAB, start by taking your 3" speed bore and drilling into the heartwood of the

The depth you drill should be determined by the size of your TAB.

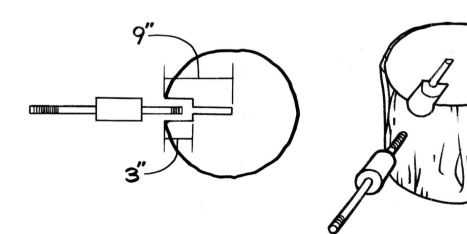

9"

3"

The TAB threads enter the tree fully, the collar or boss (3" section) enters the tree half way (depending on size of TAB), and the stem or perch (unthreaded section) sticks out from the tree and holds your beam.

tree. You should measure from the edge of the heartwood, not the cambium. Bark is soft and does not offer structural support. Look into the hole and you will see a line of color change that indicates where the heartwood begins.

- For a 1" collared TAB, you should drill 1" into the heartwood.
- For a 3" collared TAB, you should drill 2" into the heartwood.
- For a 6" collared TAB, you should drill 3" into the heartwood.

Make sure your drill is level and pointed in the direction you want it to be. Have a friend sight the bit from different angles to make sure you don't get out of level or off course as you drill. Use a magnetic torpedo level on the bit. If the bit is too short, you can use a string level (off of the string). Remember that if your tree leans at all, your bit won't sit perpendicular to the bark, even though it will feel out of level drilling this way. I recommend tying your level to your harness with a string. After dropping my torpedo

Measure the length of the threaded shaft of the TAB and mark that length on your auger bit.

level so many times I resorted to using the string level in the photo on page 80.

Once you drill your hole for the collar, select your auger bit for the threaded part of the bolt. For a soft wood like pine, use the 1" in diameter auger. For a hardwood like hickory, you may have to step it up to a 1¹⁄₁₆" bit or a 1⅛" bit. You can always go back and drill more out but you can't put wood back, so start thin if you are unsure. Measure the length of the threaded shaft of the bolt and mark that length on your drill bit.

Drill into the center of your 3" hole until that mark enters the tree and you can no longer see it. It is easier than you think to get off of level. I personally drill an inch, and then check, drill an inch, and then check it again. This way you can be certain the TAB will seat snuggly. To avoid leaving wood chips in the hole, try to pull the drill out while still running it forward. You may not have the strength to do this, in which case

you can take a small tube, insert it into the hole, and blow the chips out.

If, while you are in the tree, you are finding the large drill too cumbersome to use, try utilizing more points contact to gain stability. Hang off of your rope, stand on a ladder and attach yourself to the trunk with your flipline. Position the drill right in front of your chest and use your body as a level against the flipline. If that doesn't work, you can throw a ratchet strap around the tree and around the back of the drill. Crank it down to give you an assist until the bit is sunk into the tree.

Installing the TAB

Once your hole is drilled, you are ready to screw the TAB into place. The recommended practice is to slide your bracket onto the perch, thread the nut onto the perch, and begin by hand screwing the TAB into the hole. This way when you

crank down on the nut you don't risk not being able to slide the bracket on later on. This part can be physically demanding and take time. A hardwood can be a very tight fit, which requires a cheater bar on the end of your large pipe wrench. If you are hanging in a harness you may not have enough leverage to screw the TAB bolt in all the way. At this point, clip a carabiner through the hole on the handle of your pipe wrench and place a sling in the carabiner. You can jump on the sling to force the TAB into the tree. Make sure you are harnessed in case the wrench slips off the nut. This method will save you in a pinch, but be careful. If the wrench pops off it could hit you in the face. If you still don't have enough force, you may want to consider drilling bigger if you aren't in far yet. If you are getting closer to the end then just tie a rope onto the end of the wrench and have someone pull down on it from the ground.

You can use a pipe wrench on the non-threaded part of the bolt, which would allow you to add a bracket after installation, but this chews up the coating and can cause rust. Sometimes it's easier to put the bracket on afterwards though, such as a TAB for knee bracing. If you are installing a lag bolt, you will have to slide any bracket onto the bolt before screwing it in.

Once your TAB is secured into the tree you have made a big step towards getting lumber into the tree.

TAB accessories
The TAB bolt is only half of the equation. You can choose a sliding, floating, hanging or paddle bracket to put onto the TAB to make it useful in several ways.

- A sliding bracket is ideal for a one-tree treehouse or any scenario where you don't need the bracket to be dynamic.
- A floating bracket is ideal for mid-height treehouses between multiple trees.
- A spacer is used to keep the platform from coming too close to the bark of the tree.
- A suspension bracket is used between a TAB and a lag bolt when dealing with heavy loads. Heavy isn't very descriptive, but the makers and sellers of TAB bolts avoid giving technical specs for what I assume are liability reasons. They say the largest TAB bolt can carry a load between 8,000-12,000 pounds. I have heard this number fluctuate depending on the seller. The challenge when deciding whether or not to use a suspension bracket for your TAB lies in the fact that when you add strength (another bolt) you increase penetration of the cambium of the tree. You will have to weigh the pros and cons for your specific build. If you think you are anywhere near the working load limit of the TAB, then I would add the suspension bracket. If you think you aren't going to be that heavy then I would leave the TAB as is and avoid stressing the tree more than necessary. If you have a huge tree, then I wouldn't worry as much about the additional bolt.

To install this system you will attach a short cable and turnbuckle to the end of your TAB bolt, and run it up to a lag bolt higher in the tree. Three to five feet higher is a common installation height. This allows the TAB to hold even more weight and decreases the risk of the TAB sagging if the

A knee brace can be used to support your treehouse platform.

treehouse shifts out to the end of the perch. It also helps as the tree grows and the platform moves towards the end of the perch. Place the turnbuckle either on the bottom or the top bolt depending on which location will be easiest to adjust.

INSTALLING A KNEE BRACE

A knee brace bracket is used anytime you want to support the edge of a platform from below. This creates a triangle between the trunk and the treehouse platform and is often a necessary component of a strong foundation. There are several ways to install a knee brace, and they vary based on your skill level as a carpenter. In reality, the best way to install a knee brace is often too challenging for your average treehouse builder. Ideally, you could install the TAB bolt with knee brace paddle already fixed, and then mount the knee brace itself between the platform and the paddle. This however is difficult because: (A) you will need to line up bolt holes on the paddle; (B) you will need to get your distance between the platform and the TAB correct; and (C) you will need to account for the distance the TAB sticks out from the trunk to be able to slide the knee brace on.

When you're sitting under your tree with all the parts needed, you may visualize this task and find it easy. If so, go for it! For the rest of us, here

are a few tricks to help make this task a little more manageable.

1. Measure the distance between the trunk and the edge of the platform where the knee brace will be attached. Then measure down the trunk from the platform this same distance. This will give you the dimensions needed to create a 45° angle.

2. Mark this height and make sure you are centered on the trunk in relation to the direction the knee brace will face.

3. Install your TAB without the bracket or nut on the perch. Use a pipe wrench around the perch to tighten the bolt.

4. Measure a rough distance between the TAB and the edge of the platform. Cut your post to length.

5. Install the knee brace paddle TAB into the post. The width of the bracket is conveniently the same width as the bar of a chain saw, so this will be your tool of choice. If you aren't skilled with a chain saw be prepared with a few extra posts in case you make a mistake. Place the paddle on the outside of your post; mark the holes for the bolts and drill these holes. Slot the paddle into the post and assemble the bolts.

6. At this point you have reached the tricky part. Take measurements from the back of the perch to the bottom inside corner of your platform beam edge. This is the measurement for the mouth of your notch. Mark a 45° angle to be cut out for the platform beam to sit in. Now, this is much easier done if you are using dimensional lumber. Cutting square on a rough timber is tricky and can result in having to test fit and re-cut several times. (Rough lumber is, however, a great way to get treehouse style points). The reason this installation method makes sense is because you can take the beam on and off the TAB if you need to.

7. Assemble the entire knee brace. This will look different depending on how high up you are, but the trick is often getting the knee brace into position without weighting the platform. If you have someone standing on the platform it will sag and the knee brace won't fit, but if no one is up there to put it into place, then you won't make progress. You can overcome this in

various ways, but for me simply hanging off the edge in a harness is the best technique. You can use a rope and pulley to hoist the knee brace into place. One person can hold the weight of the knee brace while the others mount it.

Once you are happy with how your knee brace sits, and the platform meets your requirements for level, screw the knee brace in place and thread the nut onto the TAB bolt. With this TAB setup the knee brace can pivot side to side and slide back and forth. This allows for some movement but not enough if you are high up in a multi-tree treehouse.

If you are using a large lag bolt to fix your knee brace bracket to the tree, you can get away with attaching the brace at the top first, holding it in place, and drilling your hole through the bracket itself. Then you can slide your lag in and screw it into the tree. This is a quick and easy method that works well for smaller treehouses.

You can achieve strength in your platform by putting a knee brace on both edges of the platform. You can also create a spanning strut, which is an isosceles triangle that essentially combines two knee braces into one super strong supporting shape. There are many different ways to use geometric shapes to achieve your desired structural strength. Many of these methods can be taken and altered from standard construction methods. I love looking at bridges or spans for ideas. I encourage you to try to think outside the box and create your own methods. The most important thing to remember while doing this is to consider how the tree fits into the equation. For example, two knee braces would provide great strength and stability, but would they allow for enough movement between multiple trees? As always, it's about weighing the pros and cons and achieving a balance.

Installing eyebolts for cabling

If you are going to have a suspended load in your design, you will have to install the eyebolts or TAB to hold the cable before you raise the beam. If you have a short cable with a downward direction of pull, then a TAB with a suspension bracket can work great to hold the load. If the cable will pull outward on the bolt, where the load is held out away from the trunk, I like to through bolt the trunk to ensure the bolt cannot pull out. You will have to take into account the thickness of your trunk when designing because you may be working in a tree that is too thick to accept a through bolt. You will also want to make sure you have a ship augur bit long enough to drill all the way through the tree. You can also use chain as an alternative to cable.

Before drilling for your cable, think about how the cable will hang. Will it rub on any part of the tree or treehouse? Will it be in the way of the living area? Make sure the attachment to the platform isn't going to cause the treehouse to settle and swing in a direction you don't anticipate.

When you use a cable system, you need a turnbuckle. Turnbuckles allow the cable to be tightened or loosened, which is necessary when attempting to find level. Furthermore you need to make sure you buy products that are rated to exceed your treehouse loads. You will want drop forged, galvanized, shouldered eyebolts to hang your cable from. I use eyebolts with a 1" diameter. Most eyebolts are designed to have a straight direction of pull. When you pull at an angle to the shaft of the bolt, the eye can snap off. Shouldered eyebolts are the only eyebolts that are designed to be pulled at an angle. If you decide to use hardware that's not designed specifically for treehouses then you need to do your research and make sure it will be strong enough.

Cable is awesome because it is so strong yet endlessly dynamic. It is adjustable, looks good, and can allow you to give the trees a lot of room to grow if done properly. When working with cable you will need:

- An angle grinder or cable cutter designed for your diameter of cable
- Safety glasses
- A socket set
- A torque wrench and cheater bar
- Flat bars or crow bars to get leverage to turn the turnbuckle
- Cable, thimbles, cable clamps (U-bolts), turnbuckles, washers and eyebolts

Once again, I like to go big with the cable. Cable comes in a variety of coatings and weave pat-

your thimbles and cable clamps should be ½" if your cable is ½".

When you install your cable system, start with the eyebolt through the tree. I like to get everything prepped in advance so that there is minimal time struggling to assemble while hanging in a harness. You can even preassemble your entire cable through the first eyebolt before you put it in the tree. That way it is all set up as soon as it's through the trunk. You will often have to force the thimble onto the eye of the bolt with a hammer or clamp. A thimble is a curved track that you rest the cable in around bends to prevent kinking. If this is the case, make sure you do it on the ground; it will be nearly impossible up in the tree. When the time comes for assembly, make sure your U-bolts are seated correctly. The rule is "never saddle a dead horse." Although this saying doesn't do the greatest job explaining the task, it refers to placing the U side of the cable clamp in the non-load-bearing side of the cable. If you do it backwards you will risk kinking the load bearing cable. The saddle is the part of the clamp that straddles the U, and the "dead horse" refers to the dead (unweighted or slack) end of the cable. They do make cable clamps now that are the same piece on either side, which allows you to not worry about this rule.

Unscrew your turnbuckles up to the last inch of thread. This way you have plenty of room to tighten the system. It can help to drill and install your eyebolts in the beams before raising the beam into the tree. This way as soon as it's up you can thread the cables through, and weight a fully structural aspect of your foundation. Tighten or loosen the turnbuckles using flat bars for leverage to achieve desired tension and a level beam.

terns. You can choose for yourself what kind to get. As long as you select a weatherproof variety and follow the distributor's weight ratings, you should be fine. Galvanized is stronger and cheaper but won't hold up to weather as long as stainless steel. Even a cable as thin as ⅛" can have a breaking strength of 2,000 lbs. I like to use ½" cable, with the biggest turnbuckles I can find, and 1" eyebolts. Not only is this stronger, but it makes people feel good. Beefy cable just feels safe when you look at it – and if you have renters staying in your treehouses (like I do), their overall feeling of safety is key. Large turnbuckles (which are usually your weakest link) also allow you to have more room to adjust the tension. It's more expensive but it's just one less area to have to worry about. Make sure that when you purchase your cable and hardware you get sizes that are compatible with each other. For example,

CABLE ADJUSTMENTS & NON-STRUCTURAL USES

The most difficult part about working with cable comes when your design does not match the actual balance of the treehouse. You may think that the house will hang in one way, but as you build it settles in a different way. This can especially be difficult before you have something with sheer strength, such as plywood decking, holding your platform square. Part of this is unavoidable if you don't have a good design. But there are ways to be prepared for it and tackle the problems when they arise. Your first friend is going to be a set of ratchet straps. You can put slings on either corner of the treehouse frame and tighten the straps to force things into square. The bigger the frame, the bigger strap you will need. You can also use a strap running from the frame to the tree itself to move the entire platform around. Be sure to use slings so you aren't running the moving strap directly against the bark. A spud bar and blocking against the tree can also help provide a burst of force to assist the straps. Just place the long bar between the frame and the trunk to get leverage. If ratchet straps aren't

cutting it, you can use a come-along or winch to move the treehouse around.

Getting your first beams square and fastened together is one of the first big hurtles.

To get similar results to the ratchet straps, but in a more permanent fashion, you can install an adjustable X-bracing system on the under side of your frame. This isn't applicable for all treehouses, but can help in many scenarios. By fixing cables to both front or back corners of your treehouse, crossing them to create an X, and attaching the other side to the TAB bolt with a turnbuckle, you can effectively square

your frame and also put a limiter on its movement. You can tighten the turnbuckles for the early stages of construction to help keep things ridged, and then loosen them slightly to continue to allow the trees to move.

FRAMING

When you take measurements to build your frame, make sure you account for tree movement and growth. Don't measure from the tree-to-tree or else your beams will bounce back and forth between trunks as the trees sway. Leave more room than you think to account for deck over-

An example of framing around the tree.

is very attractive. The issue comes in when you start dealing with beams that are close to tree trunks. Eventually, the trees will get so big that you are looking at a complete structural overhaul or dismantling. I had to do this on my first treehouse when the sycamore outgrew my frame. Luckily it was a lightweight treehouse!

The second option can be achieved by offsetting your structural beams and running your floor joists from one (attached on the same plane) to the other (sitting on top of the beam). You would leave slack on the joists and secure them with the decking. This technique allows the joists to slide on the beam as the tree moves, but more importantly, it allows for nearly unlimited adjustment as the tree grows wider. This method will only work if the house part of the structure is far enough from the trees that you won't have to trim into the walls. This method also has a weight limit, because at a certain point the weight of your house won't allow for the joists to slide regardless if they are screwed in or not.

SINGLE-TREE TREEHOUSES

When building in a single tree, your design will look much different. In a way, it is much simpler because you don't have to worry about the different trees moving independently of each other. On the other hand it is more complex because you have a tree running through the center of your structure! There are some great designs out there that tackle this challenge. Some builders cantilever the treehouse off to the side of the single tree. Some use compression rings and cables to hang structures off away from the trunk, but still around it. And some use a sliding clamp method of framing that allows for extreme adjustability to account for tree growth.

hang. It's also important to always use screws or bolts to assemble your frame. If your structure is moving constantly, nails will eventually pull loose. Ideally, your structural beams will be far from the trunk so that over time you just have to trim away floor joists and decking. This, however, isn't usually possible. I like to trim my decking far back off the trunk (around 6") because I have seen how much trees move in a storm. I don't want my precious cambium getting smashed from all sides. If you do leave a smaller gap, say around 2", be prepared to come back with the jigsaw and trim room every year.

Two general ways to conceptualize a treehouse are: (1) build a ridged structure that moves independently from the tree; and (2) build a dynamic structure that moves with the tree and within itself. I find the first to be easier, but in some ways the second option allows for a longer treehouse life.

An example of the first method would be to build a normal deck, and hang it with cables away from the trees. To me the simplicity in this

When building in a single tree, taking tree growth into consideration is even more important. It's easy to build away from a tree on a two-tree treehouse. It is difficult to leave ample room for growth while not loading the tree up with bolts when dealing with just one tree. There are two schools of thought for design. One is to build a frame that leaves plenty of room, and be prepared to trim decking back as the tree grows. The second is to build an adjustable frame that can be moved as the tree grows. I personally really like the adjustable frames because they are more versatile. You are less likely to underestimate the speed of tree growth and have problems down the line with this method. The downside is that if you underestimate the weight of your house, you may end up with a design you think is adjustable but simply isn't due to lack of mobility.

The concept of a sliding clamp frame is that instead of screwing your foundation breams together, you stack them, and clamp or bolt them together. When the time comes to adjust as the tree grows, you simply unbolt and slide the frame outwards. You will also have adjustable legs (knee bracing) that can be lengthened to meet the platform beams. This technique can be applied exclusively in a design or partially. It can also be used on a multi-tree treehouse. This method is bulletproof except for the weight limit. As soon as you add a heavy house on the platform, the beams have the potential to be very difficult to move.

If you are just building a small kids' treehouse then you may go for the simple, shorter-lived framing option. You can achieve this by placing two beams on TABs on either side of a trunk, cantilevering them out, and framing a platform off of them. You will still need knee bracing to

Here is an example of an adjustable frame provided by Adam Mcintyre with Carey Group design by Joel Hoffman with TreeDimensional.

Notice here that the legs are telescopic. To adjust you simply loosen the bolts and slide the frame away from the trunk.

Here we used an octagon as a key stone to support the roof without making contact with the tree.

hold up the outside edges of the frame. Playing around with different shapes to fit the tree is a fun challenge.

Raising the walls

Once your platform is built, you are ready to build the room that will sit on it. In theory, this is the easy part. At this stage normal construction can ensue. As you design, don't forget to constantly keep in mind the growth of the trees. If you have the option, design a platform much larger than the footprint of the house. Not only will this give the trees ample room to move, but it will also make working on the house much easier. Putting siding up while standing on a deck is a lot easier than when you're on a thirty-foot extension ladder. A wrap around deck is also a great way to make sure you are making the most of your view!

Letting go of level

Before constructing your walls, you have to embrace the fact that this isn't normal construction. Of course, you want a level and plumb treehouse, but sometimes using a level isn't the best way to achieve this. I have been on sites where every morning I would walk up to the treehouse and swear it had shifted out of level overnight. When in reality our eyes just assume trees grow straight when they often have a slight lean. I would check level every morning and find it perfect. It was just an optical illusion caused by the organic surroundings. If you build a level platform, your walls should sit plumb on top of it. But what happens when a gentle breeze sways the tree back and forth? Levels are so sensitive even a wind you can't feel can cause the bubble to slide in and out of level. This can be very frus-

trating. I find the best route is to build everything square off of your platform. This is assuming your platform is level on a still day. If you build square then you know that as the entire structure gently rocks in the wind you don't have to worry about referencing a plumb line. You may not even have a platform to work on. Or you may be building an entirely curved structure; if this is the case then you are probably well on your way to letting go of level. Embracing the organic nature of treehouse construction is fine by me. Sometimes building by feel is all it takes to get a house in true harmony with its host tree.

A mistake I have made in the past is accounting for lots of growth at the platform but not taking into consideration that the tree leaned inwards. By the time I put the roof on I went from a foot of clearance to 3". I had to cut the overhang back drastically. You will also want to think about leverage on the house and how that will be affected by tree movement. If you have a tall house on a suspended load, any movement you make will be felt greatly throughout the house. This isn't necessarily a huge deal, but it can feel uncomfortable, especially for those who aren't used to arboreal living. If you want to make a treehouse that the general public won't have fear of, then it's best to stay below twenty feet. (Personally, I feel that treehouses are a great medium for people to find their comfort zone and step outside of it.)

Another area where finding a balance is key is the weight of your room. Obviously you want to build a room that is strong and will withstand the elements. Using common sense is your best bet at this stage. If it's considered over-engineering in normal construction, then it probably doesn't belong in the walls of your treehouse. An example

or know a fabricator. Most treehouses don't even have insulated walls or finished interiors. As you are designing the feel of the interior space, try to find ways to double the use of each material. For example, is your exterior siding pretty enough to be the finished wall of the interior? Could you take it one step further and use a structural siding that would also give you sheer strength? Maybe at that point you could turn your stud framing into built-in shelves. Is the decking nice enough to be the finished floor of the interior? These questions can be applied to furniture as well. For a "tiny home," I like to try and make each piece of furniture do two jobs. A chair can open up for storage, a built-in table can fold down for room to stretch out on the floor, and a hammock can be lifted to hold sleeping bags up onto the ceiling and out of the way.

Above left is a space efficient kitchen. Everything you need fits in one compact zone. Of course you've got to have windows so you can still check out the birds while you cook.

Obviously, these are the finer details of design; take them or leave them. The bottom line is get to know your trees. You may be building in a giant hickory that won't be phased no matter how heavy your wall materials are. Or you may be building in a tulip poplar whose branches could snap under light loads.

THE FINISHED PRODUCT

Putting the final touches on your treehouse is a bittersweet moment. The satisfaction of seeing your efforts come to life is one of the greatest feelings often lost in today's screen-based world. You can touch it, you can play in it, and you can watch your kids' imaginations light up as they climb into it. That is a great feeling. Finishing is

of a way to save on weight would be to create sheer strength within the framing of your walls instead of sheeting them with plywood. If you're building a kids' treehouse you can often get away with 2x2 studs and using a siding material that will create your sheer strength.

In the build shown we created sheer strength within the walls using 2x4s, to avoid sheeting the exterior in plywood

There are many other ways to save on weight. If you are building a sizable treehouse, and you are in a climate where moisture is not a concern, then you could replace your foundation beams with laminated veneer lumber (LVL) beams. These are much stronger pound for pound than a rough sawn timber beam. The downside is that you really cannot get them wet because it can cause the glue to de-laminate. You could also explore a lighter weight metal frame if you have the skills

also sad because the challenges are over. The dreaming and designing, and endless possibilities have come to a halt as you have made all of the necessary decisions. I truly do enjoy building them as much as I enjoy living in them.

After each build I like to walk through the finished treehouse and take notes as to what I would change if I built it again. Naturally there is always room for improvement.

I owe the carving of this beautiful door to my brother-in-law Dylan Tennison.

No matter where you are in the house there is always a view.

EMERGENCY REPAIRS

The world of treehousing isn't new, but it is unfamiliar. Because of this, we are all pioneers to a degree. When you are venturing into new territory, mistakes will be made, and repairs will be needed. If you build your treehouse and realize after the fact that you need to adjust something major, these tips may help you achieve the repair and keep your treehouse project afloat.

If you have to swap out your foundation or make alterations, the task is fairly simple: Lift the house, tie it off, and then swap the old foundation with the new. The most important step in this is making sure you are using strong enough gear to lift and lock off the weight of the treehouse. The slings you used for your rigging may be seriously stressed with the weight of the entire structure. When doing this kind of repair, redundancy is necessary. First, put temporary anchors high in the tree to run cables or heavy-duty rope down to the frame to tie it off, so it can't fall any lower than it currently sits. Then set a second anchor to attach a winch – you'll be using the winch to lift the treehouse. Make sure both the backup and the winch are rated to lift the weight of your treehouse. Once you have the treehouse lifted, you can make the needed repairs and lower the house back onto its supports. Always stay harnessed and be aware that if you are working in or under the house you could be putting yourself in harm's way if you are not very certain of your methods.

If your tree is showing signs of illness, call your arborist. There are several techniques and products used to aid trees such as fertilizations and tree growth regulators. An arborist will be able to assess the tree and likely provide it with the help that it needs. If your tree is struck by lightning or receives and kind of structural damage, then you will definitely need to hire a tree risk assessment qualified (TRAQ) professional and professional tree climber to repair your tree.

If your tree moves more than you anticipated and your structure is hitting the bark, the first thing to do is see if you can cut away whatever is hitting. A roofline or railing can be sacrificed or altered to protect the tree. If you absolutely cannot alter the structure but want to stop the abrasion you can look into using a cable system to hold the structure away from the tree. This should be a last resort because you are choosing to restrict the tree's movement in efforts to keep the house. If you just need to stop the last 3" of sway, however, this can be very effective. Just attach a cable and turnbuckle to the beam underneath the platform, and fasten it to the opposite tree with a bolt. Tighten the cable and slide the platform away from the damaged tree until the cable length won't allow enough movement for the two to hit.

THE TREEHOUSE LIFE

Some of you will be building a very small treehouses for your kids to enjoy for just a few years. Some of you may have grand dreams of running away into the forest and living in a treehouse for the rest of your days. Whichever path your treehouse takes you down, you may find yourself feeling quite at home in the canopy. I know it sounds cliché, but there is definitely a canopy lifestyle (one which I have fully embraced). I don't know what it is about trees that is so appealing. They inspire this really deep satisfaction. The way sugar maple bark feels sliding under your palm, the smell of a walnut in the fall, or finding a perfect notch to cradle your body so you can drift to sleep and not worry about falling out are all ways that trees feel cozy. Even on a dreary day at work, I'll have moments when my movement through the canopy clicks and feels effortless and playful. I can't help but feel like the treetops are a long lost home. Trees provide shelter from the sun and rain. They can keep you safe from predators lurking on the ground, even if it's your older brother chasing you down for the TV remote. I have gotten calls from customers saying how their kids haven't picked up the video game controller since their treehouse was built. This is important. We live in a time when screens are the default answer to boredom, and kids are deprived of a relationship with nature. If treehouses can act as a catalyst for the imagination and be a stronghold for our ties to the woods, then I am 100% on board. I got into sharing treehouse dreams because of the way it inspires people. I hope that this book not only inspires you but also gives you the confidence to strap on your tool belt and make your own deeply rooted dreams a reality.

useful resources

HARDWARE & SUPPLIES

U.S. Cargo Control: uscargocontrol.com
Treehouse Supplies: treehousesupplies.com
Nelson Treehouse and Supply: nelsontreehouseandsupply.com

LOAD CALCULATORS & ENGINEERING

American Wood Council: awc.org/codes-standards/calculators-software/spancalc
Treehouse Engineering: treehouseengineering.com

TREE CLIMBING & RIGGING

SherrillTree: sherrilltree.com
TreeStuff.com: treestuff.com
WesSpur: wesspur.com

ARBORIST SITE

International Society of Arboriculture: isa-arbor.com

PROFESSIONAL TREEHOUSE BUILDING HELP

The Canopy Crew: thecanopycrew.com

the canopy crew

THE SYLVAN FLOAT

During the last few weeks of living in my treehouse, I asked myself: If I could do anything I wanted, what would it be? The answer was to build treehouses and to have a creative platform where I could try a lot of different design concepts and styles. There was nowhere in the world I wanted to build more than the Red River Gorge. From that day on I started dreaming about all of the different treehouses I could create once I was ready and able. The Sylvan Float treehouse is the end product of many mornings of scribbling designs on a sketchpad after nights of lying awake in bed hashing out ideas and dreams. The goal of this treehouse was to be accessible to the general public, yet still capture the exposure and adventure of living in the trees. I wanted folks to feel cozy and nested in the treetops, and feel like the trees were like a second home. I wanted it to float through the forest like a boat. I wanted to frame organic shapes with clean lines to create a balance of canopy and modern design. I wanted it to be beautiful, yet still have an element of playfulness. I hope that as people enjoy this treehouse they will find themselves more open to wilder treehouses to come!

The Sylvan Float is my version of the perfect treehouse, but there are no strict rules to what a treehouse should look like. That's a great thing! As more and more treehouses are being built we will see all sorts of new designs and molds being broken. We reached out to our community and asked them to share their backyard treehouses with us. Here's a closer look at my finished Sylvan Float design as well as a few treehouses people have come up with across the country.

Support cables are shown in this view of the porch.

Bridge side view.

Stairs leading downhill from the treehouse.

Bridge side at dawn.

Front view at dawn.

Side view.

Enjoying the view from the porch.

Front view lit by morning sun.

Carved door with inlay.

Hammock side.

Porch roof.

Back porch view.

Porch railing detail.

robert compton

My treehouse is set among seven trees on floating platform 14' x 20'. Several 4x4 posts were added and cantilevered for added support. As you can see it's a Tudor style with two stories, post and beam construction and a cedar shake roof. There is wide board flooring on both levels, with a winding staircase connecting. Custom TDL windows open out and there's a stationary TDL freehand circular window. There's cherry paneling on first floor with a woodburning stove, backed by stone. Built-in bed on second floor with decorative surround. Also, window seat/storage box and bookcases. There's 30 amp electrical service with period lighting throughout.

justin rome

This treehouse is suspended twenty-two feet up in a secluded bitternut hickory tree outside the capital city of Kentucky. It is on a 15' x 16' platform, and other than the treated beams and floor joist, it is built out of wood that I milled up from a variety of tree species taken down by the tree service I work for. There are only three holes in the tree with eye bolts that suspend cable connected to the beams and one cedar post for the fourth leg. The treehouse moves in the wind and the suspension allows the tree to grow and move freely without obstruction. Not to mention, the view is incredible in all seasons!

The treehouse was something my family and I had wanted on our farm since we moved there when I was a kid. In middle school, I picked out the hickory tree and established a general design for the mechanics of the structure along with building a platform on the ground for a place to sit and enjoy the awesome view atop the hill. A cedar post needed to be set to catch the weight of one of the two beams that the structure is built from. At 13 or 14 years old, after digging not much more than 16" before hitting solid bedrock, my dream and enthusiasm for building the treehouse was put on the back-burner. In 2013, after the barn on the farm was nearly full with the dimensional lumber I had milled over the previous few years, a builder friend, my brother and I began discussing the idea of a treehouse and using the repurposed lumber to build it. We collaborated on a design for a while before redigging the hole and building forms for a footer to set the cedar post. My experience as an arborist and avid tree-worker combined with their building skills, and made the treehouse possible.

christopher wangro

Our treehouse is built on the side of a hill. The low side is about 8 feet up and the high side about 35 feet. We call it the SkyLounge. It's great for work, quiet contemplation, movie nights and is a lovely place to sleep. It's built to float around three trees using triple-triangle geometry. It all floats on three handmade braces, made to hold a 6x6. Each brace took two bolts, clamped in with a Garnier Limb.

glossary

Arborist – A professional in the practice of arboriculture, which is the cultivation, management, and study of individual trees, shrubs, vines, and other perennial woody plants. Hiring an arborist is highly recommended when assessing possible host trees for your treehouse build.

Auger bit – Augers are suited for boring deep holes because of their length. Ship auger bits are even longer.

Biochar – Essentially charcoal used as a soil additive. Biochar increases soil fertility and helps protect against diseases.

Cambium – A thin formative layer of tissue between a tree's bark and the sap wood that is responsible for new growth.

Canopy – The upper layer of a forest formed by mature tree crowns.

Carabiner – A metal loop with a spring gate that is widely used as component of roping systems.

Compartmentalization – A process by which trees close off a rotting or damaged area in order to protect healthy tissue.

Crotch – A fork in the tree trunk where it divides into two branches.

Crown – The crown of a tree consists of its branches, leaves and reproductive structures extending from its trunk.

Emerald ash borer – A green jewel beetle native to eastern Asia that feeds on ash species. It has become an invasive species and is highly destructive to ash trees native to North America.

Dieback – A condition in which a tree gradually dies starting from the tips of its leaves as a result of disease or unfavorable climate.

Dutch elm disease – A fungal disease that infects elm trees and is spread by the emerald bark beetle.

Flipline – Used to secure a climber to a tree, a flipline is essentially a rope that goes from one hip, around the tree, and attaches to the other hip.

Foot locking –A method used for rope-climbing that involves wrapping the rope around your foot so that you can effectively "stand"on the rope.

Friction hitch – A type of knot or device that allows you to attach to a rope while allowing for movement up and down the length of the rope, but locking in place when a load is placed on it.

Ganoderma – An untreatable fungus that attacks tree roots and can cause structural failure.

Grigri – A safety mechanism for climbers designed to pinch rope when it is moving too quickly; an assisted break-ing device.

Heartwood – The older, nonliving central wood of a tree. Heartwood is typically harder and more resistant to decay than the younger sapwood.

Hemlock wooly-adelgid beetle – An invasive insect species from Japan that threatens hemlock forests in the eastern United States.

International Society of Arboriculture – Through research, technology, and education, the International Society of Arboriculture (ISA) promotes the professional practice of arboriculture and fosters a greater worldwide awareness of the benefits of trees.

Knee brace – A brace between vertical and horizontal components in a structure. In treehouse building a kneebrace creates a triangle between the tree's trunk and the treehouse platform, creating the foundation for your treehouse.

Lanyard – Also known as a flipline, a lanyard is a specialized rope used to secure a climber to the tree.

Level – Perfectly flat; having an even horizontal surface.

Mechanical advantage (M.A.) – A measure of the amount of force gained from using a tool, machine or mechanical device.

Micro pulley – A specialized pulley used for climbing systems.

Pruning – Selective removal of parts of a tree in order to remove diseased or damaged areas, to encourage new growth or to remove limbs that pose some kind of risk.

Progress capture – The ability to hold a load in position and keep it from lowering as it is being raised. Progress capture devices include grigris and port-a-wraps.

Redundancy – With regard to climbing, redundancy is the act of using multiple roping systems or connections to ensure safety in the event of failure of a primary system.

Resistograph – An instrument that detects decay and cavities in trees and timber. Through resistograph technology, an arborist is able to detect wood decay, stages of rot, hollow areas, cracks and ring structure.

Rigging – Ropes and related equipment used for lifting and supporting loads.

Root Crown – The part of a tree's root system from which the trunk arises.

Soil compaction – Soil may become compacted due to many factors suc as a nearby driveway or vehicle traffic. This results in reduction of pore space within soil, which in turn restricts the development of a tree's root system.

Split tail – A rope with eyed ends used to create a friction based rope climbing system.

Square – Consisting of accurate right angles.

TAB (treehouse attachment bolt) – Specialized bolts engineered specifically for treehouse construction.

Tag line – A second or third rope tied onto a beam and held on the ground to control swing or movement.

Throw line – A line with a beanbag attached that is thrown over a tree branch and used to pull your climbing line up and over.

Tree growth regulator – A chemical treatment used to slow the annual growth of trees.

TRAQ (Tree Risk Assessment Qualification) – an ISA qualification program that trains arborists how to use the methodologies outlined in the ISA Best Management Practices for Tree Risk Assessment.

Turnbuckle – A device used to adjust tension in a cable-based system.

Water level – An accurate means of finding level in a natural setting, a water level consists of a clear plastic tube filled most of the way with water. Level between two points is found when the water line at each end of the tube settles.

index

acknowledgements

Photography by:
John Wesely
Kristin Guastaferro
Megan Lewin
Adam Mcintyre
Joel Hoffman
Robert Compton
Justin Rome
Christopher Wangro

Illustrations by:
Josh Raff
Nathan Maggard
Rick Weber
Heather Francis

ABOUT THE AUTHOR

Django Kroner is a tree climber and treehouse builder. Through three years of experience living in the canopy, he learned the finer details of treetop living and realized the importance of sharing what you love. Django was raised in Cincinnati, Ohio, and currently lives either there or in the Red River Gorge, Kentucky. He has a background in rock climbing, tree climbing and construction, and he founded the Canopy Crew in 2013. Dedicated to life in the trees, Django spends most of his time off of the ground or looking up. He comes from a large family of creative entrepreneurs and considers them his greatest blessing. When he's not in the trees, he enjoys spending time working with wood and leather, refurbishing his camper, exploring the local forests or flying his paraglider to new views. To find out more about his pursuits visit www.thecanopycrew.com.

Distributed in Canada by Fraser Direct
100 Armstrong Avenue
Georgetown, Ontario L7G 5S4
Canada

Distributed in the U.K. and Europe by
F+W Media International, LTD
Pynes Hill Court
Pynes Hill
Rydon Lane
Exeter
EX2 5SP

Tel: +44 1392 797680

Distributed in Australia by Capricorn Link
P.O. Box 704
Windsor, NSW 2756
Australia

Visit our website at popularwoodworking.com or our consumer website at shopwoodworking.com for more woodworking information.

Other fine Popular Woodworking Books are available from your local bookstore or direct from the publisher.

ISBN-13: 978-1-4403-4507-4

20   19   18   17   16   5   4   3   2   1

Editor: Scott Francis
Cover Design: Daniel Pessell
Interior Design: Angela Wilcox
Production Coordinator: Debbie Thomas

Read This Important Safety Notice

To prevent accidents, keep safety in mind while you work. Use the safety guards installed on power equipment. When working on power equipment, keep fingers away from saw blades, wear safety goggles to prevent injuries from flying wood chips and sawdust, and wear hearing protection. Whenever possible use push blocks and other safety devices to minimize risk. Don't wear loose clothing or jewelry when working with power equipment. Tie back long hair to prevent it from getting caught in your equipment. People who are sensitive to certain chemicals should check the chemical content of any product before using it. The authors and editors who compiled this book have tried to make the contents as accurate and correct as possible. Plans, illustrations, photographs and text have been carefully checked. All instructions, plans and projects should be carefully read, studied and understood before beginning construction. Due to the variability of local conditions, construction materials, skill levels, etc., neither the author nor Popular Woodworking Books assumes any responsibility for any accidents, injuries, damages or other losses incurred resulting from the material presented in this book. Prices listed for supplies and equipment were current at the time of publication and are subject to change.

Metric Conversion Chart

Inches	Centimeters	2.54
Centimeters	Inches	0.4
Feet	Centimeters	30.5
Centimeters	Feet	0.03
Yards	Meters	0.9
Meters	Yards	1.1

a content + ecommerce company

Ideas · Instruction · Inspiration

Receive FREE downloadable bonus materials when you sign up
for our FREE newsletter at **popularwoodworking.com**.

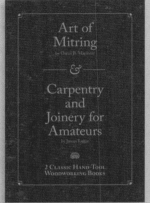

Find the latest issues of *Popular Woodworking Magazine* on newsstands, or visit **popularwoodworking.com**.

These and other great Popular Woodworking products are available at your local bookstore, woodworking store or online supplier. Visit our website at **shopwoodworking.com**.

Visit our Website

Find helpful and inspiring articles, videos, blogs, projects and plans at **popularwoodworking.com**.

For behind the scenes information, become a fan at **Facebook.com/ popularwoodworking**.

For more tips, clips and articles, follow us at **twitter. com/pweditors**.

For visual inspiration, follow us at **pinterest.com/ popwoodworking**.

For free videos visit **youtube. com/popwoodworking**.

Popular Woodworking Videos

Subscribe and get immediate access to the web's best woodworking subscription site. You'll find more than 400 hours of woodworking video tutorials and full-length video workshops from world-class instructors on workshops, projects, SketchUp, tools, techniques and more at **videos.popularwoodworking.com**.

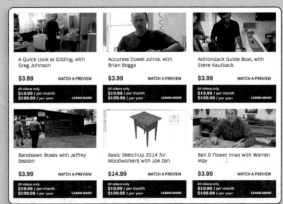